Man-at-a-Typewriter Journalism

50 YEARS REPORTING PACIFIC NORTHWEST BUSINESS

Elliot Marple

Copyright 1999 by Elliot Marple
All rights reserved.
Photo on cover and page 63 reprinted from the August 16, 1952, issue of *Business Week* by special permission © by McGraw Hill Companies.

ISBN Number: 0-9670261-0-5
Library of Congress Catalog Number: 99-93056

Design by Amy McCroskey

Published by Merrimount Press
2716 - 61st Avenue S.E.
Mercer Island, Washington 98040-2423

Printed by Gorham Printing
Rochester, Washington 98597

Other Books by Elliot Marple

Two Remarkable People,
    The Lives of Martha and Lucius Marple,
    New Englanders who settled in Seattle in 1904

The National Bank of Commerce of Seattle, 1889-1969,
    Territorial to Worldwide Banking in Eighty Years
    (with Bruce H. Olson)

Contributing editor: The PeoplesBank Story

Publication pending:

Resplendent with Promise,
    Adventures in Silver in Old Nevada,
    Letters of Samuel Hilliard Folsom, 1866-68

Episodes in Wartime Price Control and Rationing,
    A personal account, Washington, D.C., 1942-46

Contents

One	A Return to Seattle/7
Two	I Dig In/18
Three	*Marple's Business Roundup*/36
Four	The Push for Subscribers/55
Five	*Business Week*/64
Six	What is News?/68
Seven	The Changing Forest Industry/70
Eight	S.D. McFadden/76
Nine	Banks Make News/88
Ten	The Service Industries /94
Eleven	Hobson's Farm Forecast/98
Twelve	Help Wanted/109
Thirteen	A 10-Year Perspective/115
Fourteen	*Walker's Newsletter*/118
Fifteen	Rough News in Mining and Plywood/122
Sixteen	How to Take a Month Off/126
Seventeen	A Bank and its Story/129
Eighteen	Paccar Makes News/138
Nineteen	All Aboard!/142
Twenty	Scraps on the Cutting-Room Floor/146
Twenty-One	The Maturing of a Region/157
Twenty-Two	Mike Parks Takes Over/160
Appendix	Subscribers Talk Back/167
Index	175

Illustrations

Elliot Marple/8
Western Union, the way to go/25
The First Newsletter/37
How the Masthead Developed/39
Marple Gets the Story/60
Man-at-a-Typewriter: Photo from *Business Week* story/63
S.D. McFadden Ad/77
Hobson's Farm Forecast masthead/99
Parks Joins Marple/160
"The Nation's Outstanding Business Newsletter"/162
Michael J. Parks, 1999/163
Two Publishers in 50 Years/166

Chapter One
A Return to Seattle

I shall never forget the day we came into Seattle, our new home. We had been driving for a week in winter across the country, pushing through the bitterness of Midwest cold. As we came to the Rockies the weather cleared and our spirits rose. When we reached Seattle we reveled in the gentle warmth of a February sun. My wife Dot, new to the West, beamed at early signs of spring. Robins hopped about, early blossoms were breaking out, and Mount Rainier, serene in winter snow, smiled down at us. The date, February 8, 1947, is pegged in memory; it was daughter Marcia's 10th birthday.

We had said goodbye to the East and left Detroit on a Sunday at midday. Our comfortable 1938 Buick Century, bought second-hand almost 10 years earlier, was built as though for a long trip and carried two spare tires in the front fender wells. Crossing Illinois we ran into snow and bitter cold. I did not mind the snow; I was used to that. But I did not guess how cold and mean the wind would blow that night. I parked the car on the street outside our hotel. The engine had always started well in cold weather. But an unyielding wind out of Canada dropped the temperature down near zero. In the morning the engine was as dead as a block of ice. Time was precious, so I had the car towed to a heated repair garage, and before long we were on our way westward.

That was the last of our winter. Our highway across the Rockies was clear. We crossed from Idaho into Washington on a Saturday morning, a week out of Detroit. In sunshine almost warm enough for a picnic we turned off the highway to sit on a ridge above Prosser, looking out over the Yakima Valley, and had a snack. We drove on, up the deep winding canyon of the Yakima River, an exciting route I had never traveled.

We sped over Snoqualmie Pass ignorant of our luck that the pavement was bare and dry and nowhere the sign: "Chains required." It was late afternoon when the four of us—Dot, Marcia, little Sue and I—reached our Seattle destination, a rented house at 4722 Latona Avenue N.E.

The house was of stern two-story colonial-style with high ceilings, two furnaces and, we would find in the record cold of 1950, no insulation. The house nearly filled the narrow lot. A scrawny holly hedge lined the front sidewalk. But we were lucky to have a place at all. Housing was still tight after the shortages of World War II. Our friends, Lucille and Jack O'Connor, living in the O'Connor family house at the corner of Latona and 47th, had talked the owner, Mrs. Carl Reeves, into renting to us. She was moving out to live with a friend for what turned out to be nearly three years. We agreed that she could leave one of the big bedrooms crammed with the furniture that she might want again. She was just waiting. Her husband, an engineer, had skipped off to California a few years earlier with his secretary. Mrs. Reeves was sure Carl would come back; "he was a good man." But as we came to know Mrs. Reeves we had no concern that Carl would ever return.

Dudley, Hardin, & Yang - 1959
Elliot Marple

I had no job. I had just been let go at Maxon Inc., a Detroit advertising agency. I recognized that advertising was not my dish, and I was ready to leave. Now I was starting as a free-lance writer for specialty business magazines, commonly known as tradepapers. I would be paid only to the extent that the stuff I dug out and wrote got printed. We would have to live on whatever I earned at a penny or two a word. To start off, I would draw on moderate savings that we had built up in flusher times. Years later I incorporated the business and signed my own paycheck, but until then I took home only what was left in the till, and I could say wryly: "I got fired 20 years ago and haven't drawn a paycheck since." The simple truth: I survived but the Maxon agency, big in its day, went out of business long ago.

The ad agency generously kept me on the payroll for two months while I prepared for the move to Seattle. The previous summer we had taken a three-week vacation by train to Seattle and Portland. At that time I looked about a bit, but I had been in the East for 15 years and found myself a stranger in the city where I was born and grew up.

When I lost my job in Detroit, my first choice for work was magazine writing on current topics, but I saw no way to support a family before I could land even the first article. As an alternative, I kept my mind open also for work in public relations anywhere on the West Coast. In the end I settled on a slow and rocky start with tradepapers published in the East that were reaching out for news from the bubbling Pacific Northwest.

In the transition I drew on my three wartime years at the Office of Price Administration in Washington, D.C., ultimately as press chief for Chester Bowles, the head of price control and rationing. In this intensive work I came to know writers and editors of a number of business publications. Now I sent a torrent of letters to offer myself as Seattle correspondent, and I spent a week in New York going from one editorial office to another. My most important contact was Ralph Smith, editor of *Business Week*, a general magazine a cut well above tradepapers. Did he have a reporter in Seattle? Was he getting the news he wanted?

His answers were encouraging: Seattle and the Pacific Northwest had made news during the war, in aircraft, shipping, shipbuilding, and electric power. After the war, Smith thought people would leave and the region would settle back into inconsequence. But he found otherwise. People who had tasted this region during the war tended to stay, and its industries were growing. The region, Smith said, had taken on new importance. Yes, he wanted better coverage. The responsibility for Seattle, however, lay with Dick Lamb, the magazine's West Coast editor in San Francisco. See him.

I found a similar attitude with a number of editors. They were cordial—but noncommittal. Send them news and they would pay for anything they published. Roy Miller, editor of *Food Field Reporter*, a biweekly for food manufacturers, canners, freezers and wholesalers, was encouraging, pleased to widen his world. As we talked he picked from his desk a San Francisco newsletter, *Western Packing News Service*, and said of its publisher, Sam McFadden: "This fellow comes up with some pretty good stuff. If you are in San Francisco, you might look him up. He might be helpful." So it went with a number of editors. Encouraging, but not a penny guaranteed. I spent some time with Steve Rippey, Washington correspondent for a cluster of three papers in the food field.

On returning from New York I summarized for myself: "I saw some of the copy [news stories] that correspondents sent in. Why more editors don't leap in horror from the 21st floor I don't know. It is very easy to see why tradepapers pay poorly and that with good coverage and careful writing a man can make a deal for more."

I came across tracks of only two full-time tradepaper correspondents in Seattle: one for Fairchild Publications (daily and weekly papers covering department stores) and one for McGraw-Hill's tradepapers distinct from *Business Week*, McGraw-Hill's top of the line. In addition, three or four men in Seattle did some part-time tradepaper writing. Usually they worked on a newspaper and now and then rewrote small bits for a tradepaper. But they did not put on their shoes and go out and dig up something new. Part of the difficulty, I sensed, was that they did not know what the editors wanted, and the money they might get was just chicken feed, hardly worth the chase.

I did have one encouraging break in New York. *Restaurant Management* asked for a major story on Walter Clark of Seattle, newly elected president of the National Restaurant Association. I had no clue what the pay might be, but here at least was a solid assignment.

Let me go back in time. Early in December of 1946, two months before the sunny day when we drove into Seattle, I boarded a train for the West Coast. This was what the publisher Sam McFadden would call a "look-see" trip: first stop Los Angeles, then San Francisco, Portland and Seattle. Along the way I sought to learn as much as I could of West Coast business. I summed up in a letter written in Seattle on New Year's Day 1947 to Dot, waiting anxiously in Detroit. I saw three options for work: tradepapers; public relations on my own or with a p.r. firm; or public relations on a corporate staff.

In Los Angeles Ed-E Herwig, who put out a four-page weekly for the Merchants and Manufacturers Association, offered me a job, though sorry he could not pay better. That was not the work I wanted. "No, thanks!" I replied, a response that I'd repeat a number of times in the years just opening up. But I found Herwig, with his distinct first name, Ed-E, a sharp observer who liked to toss off ideas, and for many years after this visit we swapped notes.

In public relations, nowadays more nicely called communication, I found more activity in Los Angeles than elsewhere on the coast, but there were many newcomers, men just back from the war. There was a job to be done, I wrote Dot, but it would require lots of selling and months of tough work without income. I checked General Electric's San Francisco headquarters, having a lead from GE in Detroit, but found nothing.

I looked up Sam McFadden in San Francisco. He sat at an old flat-top desk in a small dark office, starkly furnished. He was in his mid-forties, unpretentious, tall, and smoking a cigar. He had worked years earlier for *The Wall Street Journal* and later headed its San Francisco office. Now he published two newsletters for the West Coast, one on food canning and freezing, the other on trucking. He had also had just started one on dairying, but within a year he gave that up. "The cows," he said, "could not read."

Yes, McFadden would like more news from the Pacific Northwest. Send down what I could, he suggested, and we'd see what we could work out for pay. He was cautious. He didn't know whether I could produce, and neither did I. As I recall, I began with him at $20 a month. Soon that became $25, later $40, and always an extra check at Christmas. Whatever he paid was far less important than his guidance, so very helpful as I built my news center in Seattle. Over the years he had greater influence on my professional work than anyone except my father.

While in San Francisco I anxiously looked up Dick Lamb of *Business Week*. We had a long talk over lunch at the Press Club. He had a stringer in Seattle, a reporter on one of the daily papers, who, however, wasn't producing much. Lamb would see what he might work out. But no commitment.

Traveling up the coast I spent several days in Portland, where my brother Warren, an economist with Bonneville Power Administration, knew the town well. I talked to a number of people in Portland. Soon after reaching Seattle I received a telegram from Quenton Cox, manager of a radio station and a leading citizen, asking if I wanted to handle publicity for the Portland Rose Festival in June. Full-time work for a few weeks, but it could be no more than a temporary diversion; no, thanks!

I had hardly landed in Seattle when Ralph Smith of *Business Week* offered me a job as a news editor in New York at "around $7,000." [To allow for inflation, multiply 1947 dollars by about eight to convert to dollars of the late 1990s.] Again it was no, thanks! Not even tempting. The West had become my dish.

By now I wrote Dot, still waiting in Detroit, that I was ready to go full-time on tradepapers. I saw two advantages: "If I do the job right,

I ought to uncover stuff worth writing for national magazines of general circulation; and if writing for general magazines doesn't work out, tradepapers should provide leads on public relations or other business activity that I might want to hop into." Down the road, I wrote, might there be a newsletter like McFadden's, or, since "business news is poorly covered by the daily papers here," perhaps a weekly syndicated column for newspapers or radio.

As January 1947 opened I scurried around Seattle searching for an office where I could rent desk space. All I wanted was a place to set up a typewriter, to receive mail, and to have access to a telephone. Mail was critical, and I needed to give eastern editors an address before they forgot who I was.

Desk space was scarce. I roamed a dozen blocks from Yesler Way up to Blanchard Street, checking mostly in older or out-of-the-way buildings where the rent would be gentle. The manager of the Burke Building at Second and Columbia referred me to a couple of his tenants. This old red-brick structure had been upgraded and renamed the 905 Second Avenue Building. I looked in on one of the tenants, Norbert Schaal, a consulting engineer. He had two rooms separated by a glass partition and three big sturdy drafting tables of his own design and make. We talked about a rental but he cautiously suggested a trial basis that was a bit too fuzzy for me. I wanted a mailing address that would stick.

A couple of days later I was pumping up Second Avenue, hat in hand on a mild day, when someone tugged at my coat sleeve. I turned around to see Schaal, short, chubby and with a question in his smile. He told me a little more of his work and what he had in mind for the office. He had a somewhat temporary job with an engineering firm in the nearby Dexter Horton Building but kept the Burke Building office for his own business. He had the help of a woman draftsman and more space than he needed. I took his offer at $20 a month, put a typewriter (borrowed from my sister Marcia) on an idle drafting table, and sat myself to work on a draftsman's high stool. I kept that office until the building was torn down to make way for the high-rise Henry Jackson Federal Office Building. Before long Schaal retired, and I bought his drafting tables that in time I found great work space for stuffing envelopes in a big mailing. Those tables have remained with the business and, recently re-covered, are still in use 51 years later.

Schaal's location, I came to realize, could not have been better. It was in the heart of the downtown business district, the financial center of the state. The headquarters of all the big banks were within easy walking distance. Across Marion Street was the Exchange Building, a showplace erected just before the turmoil of the Depression. The Exchange Building and the 1411 Fourth Avenue Building, half a dozen blocks north, were the city's prestige addresses.

Within seven or eight minutes' walk was the Olympic Hotel, the convention center of the city, and just beyond that was the blocklong White-Henry-Stuart Building, headquarters for lawyers, lumber brokers, trade associations, and a wide variety of businesses.

Four or five blocks south of the Burke Building, the Great Northern and Northern Pacific railroads had their western headquarters. The Northern Pacific was the largest tenant in the ungainly Smith Tower, which with a little generosity in the count of its tower was called 42 stories high, "the tallest west of Chicago." Within a block or two of the Burke Building were offices of most Alaska salmon-packing firms. Their principals went off to Alaska each summer for the canning season and came back seeking markets across the nation and in Europe for millions of cases of canned salmon, financed by anxious bankers.

After 10 intensive weeks of exploration I was eager to make Seattle my new base. I boarded the train for Detroit to pack up and move the family west. In the idleness of nearly four days on the train and to the rhythm of the clickety-clack of the rails I jotted down in longhand a retrospective memo that I called Full Circle:

"Fifteen years ago this week I rode the train east, fleeing the roughness & conceit of the West and the joblessness that had held me captive for 18 months. Single, I was bound for Greenfield, Massachusetts, for work at $25 a week and the security and independence that meant to a man who was broke and jobless in the midst of unemployment and despair. [I got that job by writing to the afternoon paper where I had begun as a reporter and now found it wanted an editor for a new morning mail edition.]

"Today I ride the train east again to pick up the wife I had met at Greenfield & our children, and to return west to live. I return to Seattle now with no job & wanting none, but with work — all I can do — on my own. I go out liking the West, recognizing it as home & intending to live on the West Coast permanently. What, then, is the difference from 15 years ago?

"Essentially, I think, there are two factors — confidence and perspective.

"Confidence comes from having done a job — & doing it well. It comes from being placed in a position of responsibility & meeting that responsibility fully and with recognition from those one respects.

"I left Seattle 15 years ago a shy, timid, & trembling person, having lived too long in the shelter of a family whose head neither recognized nor tolerated individuality or venturing that did not happen to meet his personal likes or habits. I may yet be shy but I have ventured and found fun & strength in those ventures.

"Those long & usually solitary walks beyond Greenfield were indeed a great venture! For by sheer physical exertion and tenacity I covered miles on little-traveled back roads, over hills and valleys and past trim farmlands. I found beauty to an extent equalled by few persons & never comprehended by those who traveled only by car. Here came exertion, exhilaration & confidence in one's physical strength. I marveled at stone walls that, disappearing in a forest, marked the edge of fields once plowed & seeded and generations later abandoned, perhaps for richer lands opening in the Ohio Valley. I carried topographic maps where a little black square located each farmhouse, now sometimes nothing more than a weed-grown cellar hole. After a day's walk I often looked up the history of villages I had passed through. There came mastery of a subject which, however circumscribed, often proved of general interest & drew one out in conversation.

"When the Depression deepened at Greenfield, I took a cut in pay and was sent across the Connecticut River to live in the mill town of Turners Falls, reporting the news of the town & handling circulation & a little advertising. I had the responsibility of directing others—a rough tough crew of high school boys who delivered the daily paper, made my small newspaper office their gathering place, and required a steady hand lest they walk all over you.

"Greenfield, Boston, and Washington, D.C. — at each I moved into work that tested a man, trained him & gave him greater responsibility. In Washington I worked with some big men — on big ideas. I may not have risen to the heights open to any one in those war days but I rose a good distance and did a sound job as I went. I hired men & women for the first time, & I am proud of the judgment and selection. I won the confidence & loyalty of my staff to a degree that touches emotion, and I won the confidence of tough, exacting Washington correspondents.

"One other factor. Through the years I have had the devotion and unflinching confidence of Dot, a factor of immeasurable importance. Soon we shall be driving to Seattle. There I shall do work, on my own, that existed just as much when I left 15 years ago as it does today. *Then* I was not capable of it; I could neither see it nor do it. *Now* I believe I can. With the very important addition of self-assurance & $13,000 in savings, I am tickled to try."

What I now visualized in Seattle was a one-man news bureau writing about Pacific Northwest business for a number of noncompeting publications, mostly in the East. I'd dig up material on a topic of interest to perhaps two or three papers and give each a story tailored to its particular field. Thus, in an early example, I hopped in the car for the hour's drive to the Mount Vernon headquarters of PictSweet Foods, then a significant packer of frozen peas and corn. For McFadden's newsletter I'd do a story on PictSweet itself—who, how, and what's new. For *Advertising Age* I'd do a story on the company's marketing. If there were new products, wider distribution, or new consumer packaging, there might be something for *Food Field Reporter* and *Modern Packaging*.

I knew the work would be heavy and the pay poor—commonly only a penny a word in tradepapers. I talked *Food Field Reporter* into doubling to two cents a word, but years later in the tumultuous changes in food marketing it went out of business. Its sister publication, *Drug Topics*, sometimes sent correspondents out to interview drug store managers on a given topic, all at a penny a word. That paper, once fat and confident, perished in the emergence of super drugstores.

Advertising Age, then and today the strongest in its field, was a strategic paper for me. I never set foot in its headquarters in Chicago. But to break into the publication I had a warm recommendation from Stan Cohen, its Washington, D.C., editor, one of many reporters I had worked with during the war. It published weekly, tabloid size on slick paper, and had space enough to let a good marketing story run long. It paid 75 cents a column-inch plus $3 for any illustration I might pick up.

Housing for the family proved difficult. Seattle was growing and had not yet overcome wartime shortage. I wanted a rental. I had no money to buy outright and no job or income to satisfy a mortgage lender. I ran ads in the local dailies, but had only one or two responses that were wide of the mark. A keen sales girl of classified ads suggested, however, that things were opening up. Her logic: room-for-rent ads were not drawing a response, and that was a sign that people who roomed were finding apartments. It was at this point that Lucille O'Connor came through with the rental of Mrs. Reeves' house.

Chapter Two
I Dig In

I wrote my first tradepaper story in Portland before I reached Seattle. I had picked up the story in Los Angeles. It began: "A weekly four-page newspaper written for labor and carrying the story of management has been launched by the Merchants and Manufacturers Association of Los Angeles."

The story went to *Tide* in New York, a monthly devoted to advertising and other communication, founded by *Time* and later sold off. I had worked in Washington, D.C., with some of the people at *Tide*. When I got to Seattle I found that *Tide* had an able correspondent so I bowed out. That proved fortunate. I took on instead *Advertising Age*, a strong publication and a leader in communication to this day. In time in the brutal competition among tradepapers *Tide* perished.

Food — its processing, marketing and distribution — soon became my busiest field. The five-state Northwest Canners Association, by good luck, held its annual convention in Seattle for three days in early January. I all but slept at the convention. I covered the speakers, two or three of national importance, got the mood of the industry and its worries, and met key people whose companies would later become grist for McFadden's *Western Packing News Service*.

The canners association, recognizing that many of its members were already expanding into frozen foods, soon added "freezers" to its name. Its annual convention alternated between Portland and Seattle, and I continued to cover these for many years, a basic source of information on a significant segment of the Pacific Northwest economy.

In the three weeks in January before breaking off to move the family west, I dug out feature stories for a half-dozen publications, including even such obscure but hungry ones as *House Furnishings Review* and *Food Topics*. In this reporting, *Advertising Age* proved pivotal. By eastern standards ad agencies in Seattle and Portland were small. Big national advertisers such as Nike, Starbucks and Microsoft were decades in the future. But there were a number of regional agencies, sometimes with a staff of no more than three or four, but alert, keen and fighting for business.

I tramped the town calling on these agencies to introduce myself and to tell them that the bible of their industry, *Ad Age,* was open for news — not fluff but solid news of marketing strategy and results. On my first call I might stir up no more than a paragraph announcing a new account, but I found at almost every agency a success story that never got into the local papers. One such was the opening of the Seattle Merchandise Mart, good for three typewritten pages that *Ad Age* gobbled up and that I wrote in greater detail for the monthly *House Furnishings Review*. I also picked up the story of the first Alaska cruise line before the announcement appeared in the daily papers.

Sometimes there was an easy brightener. One for *Drug Topics* read simply: "Shoplifting paid off at the Lincoln Pharmacy. A clerk dusting the tobacco counter found an envelope reading 'To the Owner....Here's $20, the approximate value of about eight smoking pipes that I took from your store several years ago. Just wanted to relieve a very guilty conscience.'"

Business Week remained my No. 1 target. I sent Dick Lamb a number of short items, posting him with what he could not see from his end of the West Coast. If he spotted a story he wanted from me he would order it. I think the first check I got from *Business Week* was the $10 that Lamb paid for a report on a court case in the running controversy of public vs. private electric power. The payment was nominal; I read it as saying: "I can't use this but keep trying."

A few days after I had returned to Seattle with the family and was digging into my new work, Lamb wrote of his visit to the New York headquarters: Ralph Smith the editor, Ed Grunwald the managing editor, and Lamb "talked at great length about you." [I knew Smith and Grunwald well from war days at the Office of Price Administration.] "There was nothing altruistic in our motives. We want to improve our coverage in the Pacific Northwest and think that you are the guy who can do it. To that end we want to lean over backward to make the assignment attractive to you. How we shall achieve that is something all of us will have to work out. You first of all have our pledge that we will use more copy from Seattle now that you are on the job to provide it."

Lamb spoke also of the editors' resolve "to improve the quality of our copy throughout the magazine itself.... That means tightening copy, Elliot. It means more careful reporting, more thorough distillation of all the available facts into the purest possible reading matter. This resolution bears on all of us; I am distinctly not aiming it at you or your copy, which just happens to be very smart stuff."

Later in the year Lamb broke into a note about queries I had sent him: "Now look. You've demonstrated that you don't deal in hay. Your judgment of the type of stuff we want as a normal diet is good. There's no reason why you should spend your time writing a query on a story you know we'll want and then letting the story cool until you hear from me.... When you get a story idea, take counsel with yourself, and if you decide that it's for us, write it and forget about it. I'll undertake to see that you are paid." On stories that amount to "projects" or involve significant out-of-town expense, "I think it would be well for us to continue plotting them out together."

Lamb was in effect *Business Week*'s editor for the West. He made me his man in Seattle and later for the Pacific Northwest. He was about my age, thorough and unhurried, a warm, highly competent writer and editor and a great help to me as my work broadened. We remained warm friends to the end of his days.

Lamb loved the West and refused to move to New York. Some years later he and the magazine's research editor drove from Portland to the Hanford nuclear reservation in eastern Washington. When they returned via Seattle he spoke with wonderment and awe of the grandeur of the Columbia River Gorge, his first trip through that magnificent riverway cut through the Cascade mountains eons ago.

In time *Business Week* became my biggest customer and remained so right up to my retirement some 30 years later. My first *BW* cover story was on Pacific Car & Foundry (now Paccar), builder of heavy-duty trucks. Later I produced cover stories on the biggies of the Pacific Northwest, among them Boeing, Weyerhaeuser and Boise Cascade.

Not long after opening shop in Seattle I had a lucky break. Under sponsorship of the National Association of Manufacturers, a group of businessmen put on an industrial tour for reporters and writers for national magazines. I went as representative of *Business Week*. We traveled by chartered bus on a tour extending, with breaks, for 10 days. The purpose was to show the diversity and growth of the economy 18 months after the war. The trip took us to Everett, Bellingham, Tacoma, Aberdeen, Longview and back to Seattle. We visited industrial plants, and in each city turned out to tell their story at a luncheon, press briefing or mixer. Several Seattle businessmen went along.

After the tour I offered two news stories to daily papers outside metropolitan Seattle. One was on postwar manufacturing, its diversity and vigor; the other on the timber industry and its transition to a shrinking supply and higher-cost logs. The price: $10 if an editor used my story. I made one sale, to the Vancouver (Wash.) *Columbian*. I had met several editors on the trip. When I sent out the news releases I asked whether they were interested in buying a weekly interpretive report about Pacific Northwest business. The answer: no. One editor spoke of a very tight budget, but almost all who replied were struggling with a shortage of newsprint. Charles Welch, managing editor of the *Tacoma News Tribune*, said the shortage was so severe that "we are at present leaving out...about 100 columns a week of paid advertising and an equal amount of news."

The tour, however, couldn't have been a better introduction to the state's broadening industrial base and to business leaders.

About this time two unexpected jobs came along. The Maxon agency in Detroit asked for a report on the response the daily papers gave to Gillette's Friday night radio broadcast of boxing. Maxon would pass the information along to its client Gillette, no doubt stressing what a great agency it was that could tap a seasoned analyst off in a far reach of the country. I looked on this as Maxon's generous gesture to a departed employee. It paid $50.

A bigger job was the writing of a booklet, *Tips on Trips*, for Skyway Luggage Co., Seattle. The postwar travel boom was just beginning. Henry L. Kotkins, Skyway's hard-driving president, was pushing for national markets and wanted the booklet as a promotion piece. I don't remember just how I got this job, but I think it came from my trip to Skyway's advertising agency in my introductory round for *Advertising Age*.

The booklet took endless work. To gather information I wrote airlines, rail lines, bus lines, hotel associations, and about anybody I could think of who dealt with tourists. The response was helpful. I talked with travel agents and the auto club in Seattle, and I dug out what I could at the public library. As the booklet said at the beginning, "millions of persons have a two weeks' paid vacation for the first time in their lives. Millions of old timers at travel are on the go again, but they find many changes since prewar days." The booklet suggested to travelers what to wear, how to pack, how to tip, how to travel out of the country, etc.

My work on *Tips on Trips* came in gulps, mostly in June and July — a couple of hours one day, three or four another, and 10 hours one day listed on my time-sheet as "writing and checking." The rough draft, still in my files, runs to some 50 pages triple-spaced for easy editing. I billed for 94 1/2 hours at $3 an hour plus some minor expenses, total $283.50. No fluff. Kotkins' bargain!

About this time I also wrote the lead article for *Restaurant Management* on Clark's Restaurants, Seattle. This was carefully worked out to run under the by-line of Walter Clark, president of the National Restaurant Association. When I submitted the article I told the editor it was a "difficult story from one angle: it is a success story where we dare not claim success. Essentially, this story says: if management is smart and imaginative, it can build volume and profits in spite of high wage rates. But if we say it that baldly, we put a club in the hands of union leaders all through the country to wield against Clark's fellow restaurant operators. Hence the difficulty at the wind-up of the piece, where Clark inclines to get off the track with an appeal for greater labor cooperation and where I tried to strike a compromise that doesn't seem to me effective."

To this the editor, James Warren, bounced back: "In spite of what you say about its wind-up I thought it made an excellent point." As to the text, "splendid," he wrote, "clear, convincing, constructive, and well written." He authorized payment of $100, the highest yet from any editor. I thought I had struck gold.

Shorter stories made up the day-by-day grist for tradepapers. I covered business conventions and seminars, looked in on busy committees of the Seattle Chamber of Commerce, such as on retail trade, Alaska, and industrial development. I subscribed to newspapers in outlying cities—variously in Yakima (for clues on agriculture), Spokane (for agriculture and mining), Portland (for manufacturing, shipping and agriculture), Eugene (for forest products and agriculture), and Boise (for agriculture and lumber). I carefully followed up an occasional snippet in the daily papers that looked as though there might be something significant going on.

I expanded the list of tradepapers I wrote for and before long printed in small type across the bottom of my business letterhead "Correspondent for" and a list of 17 business papers, each recognized in its specialty. The list included *Mining Congress Journal*, *Airports*, *Hardware Age*, *Department Store Economist*, *Sales Management*, *Plastics*, *Modern Packaging*, *Mill & Factory*, and so on. When I developed material that might fit a new publication I wrote the editor to introduce myself and to get a go-ahead. Even where I had already sold myself, if a story looked big, I queried first.

Space was always tight, and a correspondent like me had to produce something that would stand up in the competition for space. I tried to write in final form so that an editor could lay aside his blue pencil. I studied the tradepapers, sometimes in the downtown library, sometimes in the office of a person making news. Most often a straight news story accompanied perhaps by a handout photograph made the sale.

Sales Management, a carefully edited monthly that called itself "an idea magazine, not a news publication," asked if I might be interested in doing "an occasional article." An editor who had been on my staff in wartime Washington, D.C., had passed my name along to Ruth Hahn, the managing editor. She issued a manual for her 22 correspondents across the country and was a delight to work for.

McFadden's two sheets, on food packing and trucking, took another style of reporting. Here I wrote a memo, as precise as possible and at whatever length might be needed to give the background so that McFadden could rewrite into his unmatched prose and work in whatever else he wanted. I'll tell more later about his style.

News for *Business Week* was handled quite differently. Its correspondents, mostly full time on the staff of a bureau, submitted news in detailed memo form. The final copy, what you read in the magazine, was written in New York. There was one exception; Dick Lamb, the bureau chief in San Francisco, wrote with such clarity, precision and thoroughness that he wrote in final form, and New York editors learned to leave his stuff alone.

Business Week now and again would send correspondents a set of questions for a survey on a broad topic such as the housing market, automobile sales, or credit conditions. For this the correspondent would mail New York four or five pages that would summarize local conditions and include quotations to bring the story to life. The pay was based on the usefulness of the report. Copy mailed to *Business Week* had to have a red dot over every figure; that red dot said: "Yes, I have doublechecked this figure and it is correct."

Air mail, dependable and cheap at six cents a letter, carried most of my news to editors. Ordinary mail at three cents went by train, but with airmail San Francisco was a day away, New York two days.

The telegram was widely used when speed was critical. It preceded the telephone by decades and tied together the great industrialization of America in the late 1800s and early 1900s. The telegram remained a firmly ingrained habit with news people long after the telephone came into wide use.

Newspapers and magazines qualified for cheap rates for telegrams. The day-press rate (known as DPR) was much cheaper than a straight telegram. The night-press rate (NPR) for news sent in the

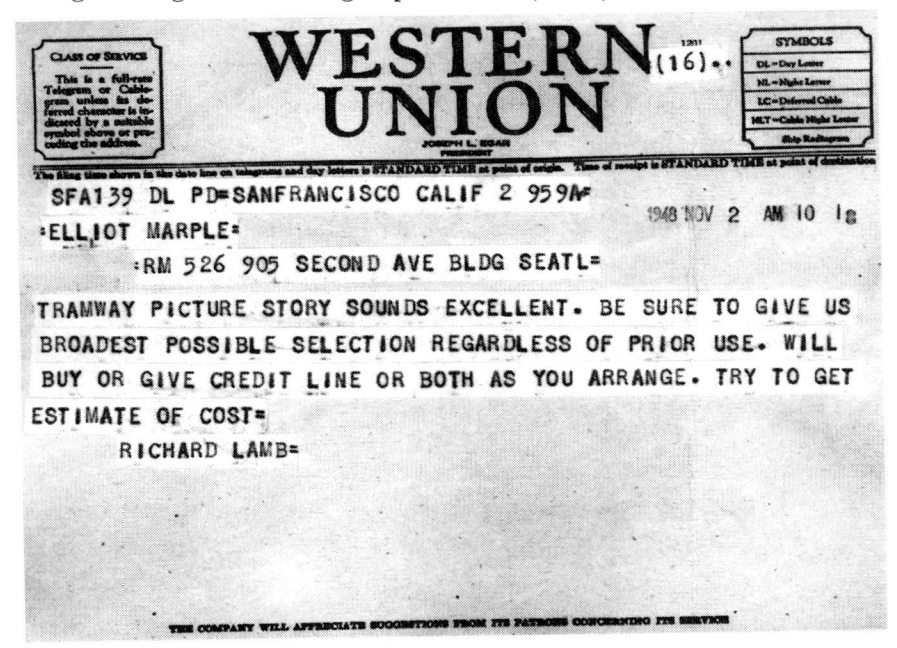

> **WESTERN UNION**
>
> SFA139 DL PD=SANFRANCISCO CALIF 2 959A=
> =ELLIOT MARPLE=
>   =RM 526 905 SECOND AVE BLDG SEATL=
> 1948 NOV 2 AM 10 18
>
> TRAMWAY PICTURE STORY SOUNDS EXCELLENT. BE SURE TO GIVE US BROADEST POSSIBLE SELECTION REGARDLESS OF PRIOR USE. WILL BUY OR GIVE CREDIT LINE OR BOTH AS YOU ARRANGE. TRY TO GET ESTIMATE OF COST=
>   RICHARD LAMB=

Western Union, the way to go

slack night hours was half the day rate. My *Advertising Age* file is sprinkled with short DPR requests from the editor such as asking for illustration to go with a story just received by mail, or a request for special coverage.

When time was critical *Business Week* wanted material sent NPR, and never mind that the material might run to a half-dozen pages, or more. Western Union had a few no-nos that we had to skirt. Ed Grunwald, managing editor, tucked this note onto his monthly report to correspondents: "If you get a telegraphic query from BW asking for 'supplementary narrative,' for heaven's sake don't wonder whether we have gone nuts. I repeat: 'supplementary narrative' is a code-word meaning 'pictures.' Often a narrow-minded telegraph office won't accept the word 'pictures' under press rates, claiming that pictures aren't press stuff. Hence the phrase — which always gets by."

As an indication how the habit of a telegram hung on, when the five-month strike at Boeing ended late in 1948, Boeing recalled the first 2,200 workers by sending a telegram to each — faster and easier than setting up a battery of people to dial the telephones.

My office, always in older buildings where the rent was cheap, had two buzzers on the wall, one for Western Union, one for Postal Telegraph. The buzzers carried a signal by wire to the downtown office a few blocks away. The system was obviously devised before the telephone came into general use. When I had a telegram to send (it always went collect) I turned the Western Union buzzer and soon a messenger arrived to pick up my story. The Postal Telegraph buzzer was dead. So was the company; it had lost out in the competition.

Incoming telegrams were delivered by a messenger, an underpaid poor devil, not always young and not looking very bright, who rode an old bicycle from the downtown Western Union office.

In the early days Seattle had two telephone systems, competitive, and if you were on one system you could not call anyone on the other. The quality of telephone communication improved, but long-distance phone rates in the 1950s and '60s were still high. McFadden used the phone with great care. He would phone when he had a hot tip for me to run down and was smack on a deadline. His call seemed to go bang, bang, bang, and he had said what he wanted and was off the line in 30 seconds. I never knew anyone who could get across so much in so short a time. But when you are paying the phone bill yourself, a dollar saved on long distance is a dollar in your pocket at the end of the day.

In my reporting, I found that sources were much more willing to open up in a face-to-face interview than on the telephone. That was one reason why as a total unknown, especially in my early work, I buttoned up my coat and went out to talk to people rather than make a cold inquiry by phone. I recall walking over to Seattle-First National Bank's head office to talk to Robert Beaupré, a senior vice-president who was a key source for a bit of industrial news just breaking. When I came in Beaupré almost exploded: So-and-so from *Time* (the magazine then had a full-time correspondent in Seattle and was working the same story) "had been on the phone for 40 minutes pushing me for information and did not have the courtesy to come to see me."

I learned. Later in my work with the newsletter I might telephone to a news source in Portland and press for detail but only if I had first met the person. Even so, I kept the call brief and often followed up with a thank-you note. But times change. Today the telephone is a reporter's most important tool and saves a lot of walking.

Lots of work, lots of fun getting to know the region, the economy, and the people who made it tick. But not much money. That was the story of my first two years in Seattle.

Payment from tradepapers was slow. I used to figure that I wrote something one month, it got published the next month, and I got paid the third month. I didn't mind waiting. It's just that there wasn't too much to wait for. At a penny or two a word it took a lot of squibs to keep the family in milk and hamburger. A typical payment voucher for one month shows that six items in *Drug Topics* earned me all of

$4.58. *Food Field Reporter*, a fortnightly, published 11 items that month for which it paid $27.32. For reasons not now apparent it also paid me $12.42 added to the $8.26 of the previous month for news from the Northwest Canners Convention. I had talked the editor into raising my pay from one to two cents a word. He no doubt regarded himself as extravagant. His publisher, in turn, must have smiled at this generosity as he smugly dressed for Sunday church, but I survived and his publication didn't.

Business Week, far and away my most important outlet, paid much better and it paid for anything ordered whether published or not. Quite early Dick Lamb saw to it that I was put on the retainer list: a guarantee of $100 a month, soon raised to $125 and later $165.

Advertising Age in Chicago was my next largest customer. It called itself "the national newspaper of marketing." I found it an alert, savvy publication. In time it not only left some of its competitors drowned in oblivion but its parent, Crain Communications, expanded with business weeklies in Chicago and several other cities, a pioneer in this specialty.

My man at *Ad Age* was Sid Bernstein, its editor and later for many years its publisher. I never met the man, but we were soon on a first-name basis. I worked closely with him, kept a flow of suggestions and queries going to him, and drew a warm response. At the outset he suggested that with an occasional feature—that is, a longer off-beat story—I should "net $90 or $100 a month, or more." But, plug as I might, I fell far short. In the first five months I earned from him $19.69, $35.84, $47.44, $37.32 and $28.32.

I wrote Bernstein in August of my first year in Seattle that I was concerned whether I could put so much time in on *Ad Age*. I mentioned that I had "used spare time to make the rounds of local agencies and advertisers, but I had gone only about half way around when I developed such a backlog of tradepaper work that I haven't yet hit a half-dozen agencies of importance."

I included in my note the reaction of a news source, Gordon

Gemeroy, who created puzzle contests and promoted them in newspapers, and I wrote a detailed story for *Ad Age*. I told Bernstein: "Gemeroy asked me, after his story came out, how much I would get for the job. I told him that at space rates for the longest story I have had in *AA* it would come to maybe $17. Later he sent a check for $25 and a note, 'Thank you for a real good job of writing.' Being a simple guy, I returned the check because I wanted to be completely free of obligation to news sources and because I hope to turn his material to further use." Then I added in pen this burr: "But I did not send it back because I felt overpaid."

Bernstein replied: "I don't believe there will ever be a too terrific volume of material out of Seattle for us, but as I told you, I think you are doing a good job, and I want to have you keep with us. Suppose that starting September 1, you add $20 to your string each month, as a 'service charge.' This still won't make you rich, but it probably will pay for postage and maybe a couple of dollars over to help out with telephone calls and rent."

Seattle was still something of a backwoods, limited in potential for national news. About the time of this exchange Bernstein wrote: "I think you have done a swell job...and my regret is that you didn't decide to locate in Los Angeles instead of Seattle, because I think I could keep you fairly busy down there." A year later in closing a letter on something else he added this p.s. by pen: "Are you wedded to life in the Great Northwest, or is there a possibility that you might come back this way some time?" He probably had a vacancy on his Chicago staff. No, thanks!

My bank account, business and personal, all in one for many years, was at Pacific National Bank, just across the street from where I had desk space. Pacific National's reputation was as a bank for business, and it was sometimes incorrectly called the Boeing bank. While other banks were adding branches right and left in a fight for size and diversification, Pacific National took pride in having no branches—at least not for many years. It concentrated its talent under the watchful eye of its president, Charles Frankland, and all the staff was right there, ready for whatever help a customer might need. The top officers, sitting at desks behind an unobtrusive railing on your right as you came into the bank, might wave to you as you walked by, reminiscent of an old-time country bank where the president knew and greeted all the customers.

I opened my account with funds from my last job in Detroit. But it was several weeks before I made a deposit from my new business. My first check from a tradepaper was from *Hardware Age* for 70 cents, and I can't for the life of me recall how I qualified for that munificence. Next came $20 from McFadden for January. I waited two weeks to take the money to the bank until I had McFadden's $20 for February and a total of $54.90 in five checks. I was uneasy that I might see in the face of the teller a smirk: "Is that all? Why bother?"

But bother I did, a lot. I very quickly fell into the pattern that held for some 40 years — work days that stretched into the evenings, and a full day Saturday, the cleanup for the week that would land my stuff on the desk of an editor in New York, Chicago or San Francisco when they hung up their jacket for work Monday morning.

Writing for tradepapers sometimes brought a bitter laugh. I had not been in Seattle long when *Food Topics*, responding to my query, ordered a merchandising story about the Bellevue Food Center, "for the very next edition." I hopped over to suburban Bellevue and hired a photographer as directed. He sent his bill to New York and was paid. I was never paid, nor was the story used "in the very next edition" or any other edition. Nor would either of two editors answer my vigorous squawks.

A year passed, and then, strangely, the paper ran the story exactly as I had submitted it and without checking for an update. But by now the figure on the store's annual volume was 15 months old, and so were the details of store innovations. There was one hitch: Some months after I sent the story in, one of the owners whom I quoted smashed into an abutment on the floating bridge to Seattle and died. In time, *Food Topics* also died. I never got paid, so I took off my income tax — erroneously, I realized later — $35.40, the pay I should have got for the story and for arranging for pictures (never used). That year I also took off $50 for a story ordered by *Housing Progress*, which went bust.

Gradually I shucked off the poorer-paying papers and put the emphasis on writing for editors who wanted judgment and analysis — something more than routine news.

I did a number of articles for *Sales Management*, "the magazine of modern marketing." It had a dozen correspondents around the country. Its initial letter to me set out that it paid on a fee basis: "The factors considered in setting prices are: Value of the story to our field, whether you had to check one source or many, how well the story is illustrated, how logical the story is organized and written. We don't pay on a space basis. We would rather pay more for a tight, complete story than for a needlessly long one." That is the sort of scope and judgment that turns a reporter's work into fun.

My first story for *Sales Management* fitted into the magazine's perceptive series on Why Salesmen Join Unions. My account focused on the union of Seattle automobile salesmen. Some time later with an order from *Sales Management*, I drove to eastern Washington and Richland, Kennewick and Pasco, adjoining cities on the Columbia River that were emerging as the Tri-Cities. During the war they supported the top-secret Hanford nuclear project. Now *Sales Management* wanted an economic profile of the emerging area. Of that article the editor of the *Tri-City Herald* wrote *Sales Management*: "I think Elliot Marple has done a swell story....He is to be congratulated." To that the editor added: "I think so too."

Business Week also was intrigued by what was stemming from Hanford, and in the course of a half-dozen years I made several trips to the Tri-Cities, a couple of hundred miles east of Seattle where, in further diversification, the flow of Columbia River irrigation water was turning a desert into miles of lush, green farmland.

Early in my work for *Business Week* Dick Lamb assigned me to a story at Medford in southern Oregon, even though that was closer to him in San Francisco than to Seattle. The story centered on Harry & David, a firm gaining a national reputation for its production and marketing of gift packages of fruit.

On the way I stopped in Portland and Salem for other news. The backup for my income tax indicates that I developed stories on that trip also for *Advertising Age*, *Food Field Reporter*, *Produce News*, and McFadden's *Western Packing News Service*. My father joined me on the trip. We were away six days, partly because persistent late-autumn fog laid a blanket of silence over the Medford airport and gave me a worrisome time getting the photographs and story off for a tight deadline in New York.

To supplement the day-by-day items of news I reached out to find new publications for feature material. *Flying* magazine took a story on Aerocar, a combination of a small private plane and light auto. It was an intriguing vehicle built by Moulton Taylor in Longview, Washington. His hand-made prototype did indeed travel on highways and in the air and was certified by the Civil Aeronautics Administration. But try as Taylor might at home and in Detroit he never found a manufacturer.

Popular Science, *Popular Mechanics*, *New York Journal of Commerce*, and *Airports* all took stories. So did *Modern Packaging*, which relied on me for a review of West Coast developments in food packaging. *Kiplinger Magazine* paid $100 for a story. I sold a couple of Sunday features to the *Seattle Times*, but at $25 each I could do no more for that paper than a fast rewrite of material already at hand. I shipped queries to *Saturday Evening Post* and *Colliers*, the leading popular magazines of the day; no sale. Their publishers were scrambling to stay alive. *Colliers* died. *Saturday Evening Post* survives but in little more than name. *Science Illustrated*, a new McGraw-Hill publication, before long gave up.

In August of 1948 I wrote my first cover story for *Business Week*. It was on Pacific Car and Foundry and its president Paul Pigott, who was moving the company from the steel business into the design and manufacture of Kenworth heavy-duty trucks. The company, known today as Paccar, operates world-wide. Peterbilt is one of its truck divisions.

The company was new to a national audience, and the story went well. There was only one hitch. For the color cover to illustrate the story the magazine sometimes splurged and commissioned an artist to paint a portrait of the president and to add a symbol of the business. The artist worked from a color transparency of the president. That part went well, and in the background a Kenworth truck rumbled out of the woods with a great load of logs. But oh, my! Look closer at those logs — not the tell-tale red-brown of western Douglas fir and cedar, but an incongruous light gray of eastern hardwoods. And at that early time Kenworth trucks were marketed only in the West. After the story was published I was supposed to present the painting to Pigott. I ducked that assignment, gave the painting to the advertising manager, and never heard of it again.

Early in 1949 Dick Lamb sent me a quick note: "Are you irrevocably committed to living in Seattle? If not, have you ever thought of Los Angeles? If LA has any appeal, how much salary would it cost McG-H to install you in our office there to cover for *BW*, *Aviation Week* and *Science Illustrated*?

"Something of that sort is taking shape in the minds of people back East. I explored the ground for them last week....The woods are full of candidates. But you will appreciate that the job calls for rigid qualification in the man — not the least of them being the power to see through the mirages that float in from the desert." I gave Lamb an overnight reply of probably no, thought about it for a day, talked with Dot, and wrote: "It's No on LA." By now my roots had taken hold in the Pacific Northwest.

Earnings from business writing were slow to build up. For the first full year my income tax return listed publishers' payments totaling $2,398.65 (and that included reimbursement of expenses for out-of-town travel). The next year, 1948, looked a little better; publisher payments came to $4,215.53 (including $196.77 for expenses). The family lived frugally. Dot, a wonderful pianist and skilled accompanist, was a good household manager. But for two years in a row I cashed war bonds and drew down our savings so we could eat and pay the rent. Clearly, I needed another publisher, one who could publish my stuff right here and pay more generously. Could I be that publisher?

More and more I had been turning over the possibility of starting a business newsletter for the Pacific Northwest. If a story was worth 500 words in New York, it surely was worth something right at home. The *Seattle Times* had not even one reporter assigned to business, in contrast to something like an unbelievable 18 or 20 today. At the *Seattle Post-Intelligencer* old Fred Niendorff sometimes pounded out a column on business without stirring from his desk. The scrappy Portland papers, the morning *Oregonian* and evening *Oregon Journal*, did better; but the *Oregonian* did not begin to have the business staff it has today, and the *Journal* did not survive the death of its very capable publisher, Phil Jackson.

In Seattle the daily stock market and a tip of the hat to the commodity market and ocean shipping seemed to be the formula for business news. But I saw business news as a great deal broader — as the story of an economy growing, diversifying, and offering new opportunities and new jobs. It would tell of expansion in the industrial base, of new companies and new ways of doing business. It would help people spot what was happening in their own backyard.

That could be an exciting story, but how tell it? In a magazine? Hardly; a magazine would take capital that I did not have and would require an advertising staff that I could neither afford nor take time to supervise.

The alternative I saw was a newsletter, the shortest route (in the days before the computer) from typewriter to reader. Here the highest proportion of effort goes into editorial content. But a newsletter, I would learn, was a medium deceptively simple in appearance and a tiger to master.

For guidance, I talked to anybody I could find who had looked into publishing a regional newsletter. One such was Dudley Ross, a San Francisco free-lancer to whom I gave the California end of an assignment from *Modern Packaging*. Ross said that he had "looked into the possibilities in this area quite a long time ago and came to the conclusion that it's an awfully long shot. Frankly, I doubt if you could make any money out of it and you might lose a chunk. It's a mighty hard thing to sell. There have been some attempts in California that failed abysmally. You may know of the most recent; a research man named Klaus, with apparently a good background, tried it out of Los Angeles. He's finally given up. I suspect it cost him a good deal, and he worked hard at promoting it.

"Regular publications and newspapers skim the cream off the top of trend stuff (admitting that it is a mighty thin job), but the average businessman won't go any further except to read the publications in his special field. Kiplinger gets away with it because Washington is a terrifying mystery to businessmen."

Ross's conclusion: "Drop it. Even further surveying can be costly, particularly in time lost from paying activities, as I have found to my sorrow in a couple of instances."

Chapter Three
Marple's Business Roundup

I could not shake the newsletter bug. I began to gather data for broader writing about the economy that a newsletter would require. I got on mailing lists for the breakdown that each state publishes weekly and monthly on employment. Here were clues on the ebb and flow among 30 or 40 categories of industry and trade. I also began building files on major companies and industries, background information that might some day prove valuable. I was committed in heart to the newsletter. I had not set a starting date, but I went about the preparation, step by step, expecting that some day a newsletter would emerge.

Right off I pegged the frequency at once every two weeks; that was often enough for a one-man shop. That production schedule would leave a week or more to gather material, Saturday for a rough draft, and Monday to revise and rewrite for clarity and condensation to space available. And the Sunday in between? I little visualized how often the typewriter at home would have to finish what wasn't roughed out on Saturday.

The letter would be printed and mailed on a Tuesday for delivery Wednesday; I was not going to compete for a subscriber's attention on Monday morning when the popular *Kiplinger Washington Letter* arrived. The masthead, a distinctive maroon, was printed in advance for a number of issues. The paper was ivory in color to stand out on a busy subscriber's desk.

The name gave me great trouble. It had to be concise and distinctive. It had to specify "business" and "Pacific Northwest" as distinguished from the plain Northwest synonymous with Minneapolis. Somehow I wanted also to suggest a look ahead in the economy.

Marple's Business Roundup:

WHAT'S AHEAD in Pacific Northwest Business
A NEWSLETTER PUBLISHED FORTNIGHTLY BY ELLIOT MARPLE & ASSOCIATES
905 SECOND AVENUE BUILDING · SEATTLE 4 · WASHINGTON · MAIN 0155

APR 13 1949

HOW'S BUSINESS?

    <u>Most striking fact</u> is gain in business activity. It's seasonal, yes, but more than seasonal. There are weak spots, undertainty, lack of confidence. Yet for region as whole, there's more work, more business.

    <u>Note employment trend</u>: In all three states - Washington, Oregon, Idaho -- claims for unemployment insurance shot up to mid-Feb. peak. Now decline has been just as sharp, just as spectacular.

    In Wash.-Ore., <u>new claims</u>, the important guide to new unemployment, are down to last year's level.

    <u>But keep this caution in mind for</u> the long pull: While employment is back to levels of year ago, there's also more unemployment. Why? Normal growth in labor force, plus people still migrating to NW. Continued growth requires expanding industry.

    <u>Now note bank debits</u>, a quick guide to changes in business activity. Federal Reserve figures this week show March debits for key NW cities slightly ahead of year ago. That reverses Jan-Feb. trend.

    Portland debits were up 1½% in March over year ago. Spokane, Yakima, Walla Walla, Boise together gained 7%. Losses were at Eugene, and on Puget Sound rim. Seattle down nearly 2%.

    <u>In department store sales</u>, entire West Coast lags behind U.S. San Francisco area best on coast, compared with '48. Seattle 2nd.

    Apparel manufacture is up seasonally. Furniture, too. Aluminum production back to peak as water power increases. But metalworking in Puget Sound cities is off and there's little near-term indication of pickup. Construction improving.

    <u>Douglas fir logging and lumber</u> are picking up fast. Seasonally logging drops some in winter but <u>mills continue</u>. This winter, severe weather hit logging hard, and weather and soft markets cut mill activity.

    You get an idea how severe the cutback was from this: Unemployed loggers and millhands received 43% of all unemployment compensation in Oregon in Jan-Feb-Mar., and nearly 24% in Washington.

The first newsletter

    Confident now of at least making a try, I worked out with an able commercial artist the design of the masthead. But from the outset this spelled trouble. I intended "What's Ahead" in dominant type to be the title, but it gave no clue as to contents, and I found people calling it by the secondary line, "Marple's Business Roundup." Before long I revised the masthead to give those three words the emphasis of the title. But what's a Roundup? Too loose a term. Some years later a respected non-subscribing businessman to whom I was talking remarked: "Oh, I thought you ran a clipping bureau." That implied that I just clipped news items and sent them out undigested. There could have been no worse put-down. That finished it! I changed in 1964 to the name that has held ever since, *Marple's Business Newsletter*.

The first issue came out April 13, 1949. I have never forgotten that date because I did forget to type the date on page 1. The error glared at me as soon as the newsletter came in from the printer. I dashed out to buy a rubber stamp and hand-dated each copy, all 500.

I had hurried the start of the newsletter because my father and mother would be returning soon from their winter in California. Father was opposed to a newsletter and thought I should write a book on Alaska. I had no money for that but wanted to plunge ahead on the newsletter without having to pick my way past nay-saying.

That first issue set the pattern. Page 1 under the heading of "How's Business?" took a broad look at Pacific Northwest business — up, or down, and why, based on interviews and such statistics as might be pertinent. Inside pages tackled a development of regionwide consequence; this first issue talked about the impact of rising freight rates. The letter finished off with shorter items spotlighting who was doing what, items that often spilled out of my reporting for tradepapers.

At the outset I had no subscribers. No, that's an overstatement. I had one, Dick Lamb, who followed with great interest what I was doing and took pride in calling himself, then and ever after, the No. 1 subscriber.

I had no money to spare for advertising and did not even think to send a news item to the daily papers. Instead, to a list of key business people I mailed a copy of the newsletter, a one-page sales piece, and

Man-at-a-Typewriter Journalism 39

Marple's Business Roundup:

WHAT'S AHEAD in Pacific Northwest Business
A NEWSLETTER PUBLISHED FORTNIGHTLY BY ELLIOT MARPLE & ASSOCIATES
905 SECOND AVENUE BUILDING · SEATTLE 4 · WASHINGTON · MAIN 0155

Marple's Business Roundup:

WHAT'S AHEAD in Pacific Northwest Business
A NEWSLETTER PUBLISHED FORTNIGHTLY BY ELLIOT MARPLE & ASSOCIATES
905 SECOND AVENUE BUILDING · SEATTLE 4 · WASHINGTON · MAIN 0155

Marple's Business Roundup:

WHAT'S AHEAD IN PACIFIC NORTHWEST BUSINESS, A FORTNIGHTLY NEWSLETTER
FOUNDED 1949 BY ELLIOT MARPLE, 905 SECOND AVENUE BUILDING, SEATTLE 4

Marple's Business Newsletter
COVERING THE PACIFIC NORTHWEST SINCE 1949

PUBLISHED ALTERNATE WEDNESDAYS BY MARPLE'S BUSINESS ROUNDUP, INC.
COLMAN BUILDING · SEATTLE WASHINGTON 98104   622-0155

Marple's Business Newsletter
Covering the Pacific Northwest since 1949
Maritime Building, Seattle, WA 98104   206/622-0155

Elliot Marple   Michael J. Parks

Marple's Business Newsletter
Covering the Pacific Northwest since 1949
Founded by Elliot Marple
117 W Mercer St Suite 200   Seattle WA 98119-3960
Telephone 206 281 9609   Fax 206 281 8035

Michael J. Parks
Editor and publisher

How the masthead developed

an order form on a self-addressed penny postcard. How many would order? I waited and wondered. A return of one to two percent in direct mail was considered good. But my market was small. I had to do better. Did I dare hope for 10 percent? Before I had any clues from the first issue I had to start work on the next issue and at the same time keep up a flow of news to tradepapers that alone paid the bills.

The answers to that first issue came back within a week. Out of a mailing of 475, I got orders from 20. They were cautious; 17 took the special rate of $2 for two months, three the full-year at $13.50. The return of new subscriptions came to a bit over 4 percent — not what I had hoped for. There was nothing to do but keep on plugging. *Business Week* carried a short news item out of which came 25 or 30 requests from around the country for a sample copy. I followed these up with an individual letter and subsequent samples but got no orders. Some were from companies interested in business in the Pacific Northwest, but some were as unlikely as the Carnegie Library in Pittsburgh and an individual in Boston dreaming about moving west "in a year or two." A writer in Washington, D.C., offered to be my Washington correspondent, and a fellow in Illinois, "not a huckster," wanted job leads and enclosed a dollar "for a secretary's time in doing me a favor."

The pattern of promotion, however, was established. For each issue I sent out 400 to 500 sample copies with a single-page sales letter and an order form. The prospect lists were gathered from directories, chamber of commerce committees, registration at conventions, names in business news — wherever I could pick up the name of an individual and his or her company. A prospect who did not order got another sample six months later.

Compiling lists was a tedious, never-ending chore. There was no computer in those days. I used a 3x5 file card for each prospect, stamped on the card the date of each mailing, then typed the address on an envelope. Later as the lists grew I typed gummed labels and used carbon paper to make four copies at a time. Still no office help.

Special mailings worked well. The Association of Washington Industries tucked two successive issues into its own mailing to members, a few of whom had already subscribed. Then I followed with a sales pitch. Out of 410 mailed to this group I got 36 subscriptions, a return of almost 9 percent. Although offered a half year at exactly half the full-year rate, almost as many ordered for a full year as for a half year. The response to that mailing "lifted me out of some despondency."

I sent four successive issues to 135 small banks in Washington and Oregon and drew immediate orders from seven (I cannot now put my finger on the final total). I bought a rubber stamp, "Last Sample Copy," that seemed to help. But a mailing to 100 "good names" in San Francisco and Los Angeles — banks, manufacturers, distributors, etc. — fell on its face.

I also used questionnaires to search out what subscribers and non-subscribers wanted.

The layout of the letter — how to make it attractive and distinctive — I was forever working on and was always looking for ideas. Right off the bat McFadden suggested, "Put a map of Wn Ida Ore up at the top to identify the area. Its sort of cold without it." Easily and quickly done — as soon as I had used up the preprinted headings. McFadden had long carried in his two publications a tiny outline map of his West.

McFadden later pushed me to stress my name in the title. That was how the sheet would become known, he said, and wished that he had gone that way himself. For transition I placed a small inset of my photo just below the outline map. Later I had the heading redesigned to incorporate the outline map and photo. The top line *Marple's Business Roundup* came out bolder and *What's Ahead* a little softer.

Of course I retained the line "published ...by Elliot Marple & Associates." And who, you ask, were the associates? Can't one dream? I hoped that now and then I might swap news with fellow free-lancers in Seattle and Portland.

At the outset I sent a copy to a number of friends around the country. I was proud to let them know what I was doing, but I was also on the lookout for ideas. Some of the most productive comment came from Oeveste Granducci, who was on the staff of the *Kiplinger Letter* when I was in Washington, D.C. He was tall and dark, a sharp observer whom I often talked to when he made his rounds for news on wartime price control and rationing.

By now Gran had left Kiplinger to set up his own shop making film scripts for business. Responding to my first issue he wrote:

> I feel, Elliot, that there's one thing of importance lacking in this issue - the meaning of what you say - the business meaning that is - what is the interpretation - how will it affect businessmen, etc., etc., etc. If you make your Letter a straight fact sheet, which I can see you're trying not to do, you're sunk. So dig like hell for the meaning of everything and be sure to include it in your Letter - even at the expense of some additional facts.
>
> In a Letter like yours it isn't brevity alone that does the job - it's clarity, clarity, clarity!...
>
> Just as a suggestion (because I know it works) let the office boy read your Letter before you publish it, and if there is something in it he can't understand you better re-write it so he can....
>
> Well fellow, you asked for it. I'd sure love to talk with you about the whole thing for I feel quite confident that you're starting in the right direction.

Two weeks later an offhand suggestion from Granducci led to the newsletter's distinctive format. He wrote:

> *While glancing through your May 11 issue, I had an idea - indirectly suggested by a recent report on the forms of business correspondence. Inasmuch as you (and I also) feel that it would be desirable to get away from the "Kiplinger appearance", what would you think of paragraphing your letter like this:*

The subject matter of any paragraph should "stick out," and one of the ways to make it stick out is - of all things - to stick it out! The whole page written in paragraphs like this would certainly change the appearance of the page a hell of a lot - wouldn't you say?

The main thought could very easily be underscored and "stuck out" like I'm doing here.

The secondary thought could then be indented and not underscored - like in this here paragraph.

> *Oh, hell—it was an idea, anyway. The main thing I wanted to say was—how's it going by now?*

I grabbed Granducci's idea, and that style has held ever since. It is not a gimmick of typography but a style that forces clearer writing — start a paragraph with a strong idea and give that idea the emphasis that comes naturally at the start of a sentence. Thank you, Granducci, good friend from the days of overworked war agencies!

Granducci came back a couple of issues later with a refinement I should have seen myself:

> *Just as a suggestion, try starting your underscored paragraphs - as often as possible - with the subject. For example, you write,* "In Western Washington and Oregon, *more logging camps are closed.*" *Try it this way -* "More logging camps are closed, *in Western Washington and Oregon.*"

How to price the newsletter troubled me from the start. Before launching the letter I visualized a price somewhere between $12 and $14. I figured $15 was out of reach. Kiplinger, so widely read, charged $18 but published every week while I was every other week. Weekly magazines, as I recall, were around $10 a year. I had about concluded to charge $14 when I got cold feet and cut to $13.50, and that was where I began.

This drew frowns from Granducci: "Pricing a direct mail deal, Elliot, is a ticklish business. I happen to know that $13.50 is a bad direct mail price. Sounds like bargain stuff. Make it a round number - $13 or $14, but preferably $15."

I hung onto $13.50 for a couple of years, much longer than I should have, concerned at one time whether I ought to drop to $12. Finally I went to $14, and over the years to keep up with inflation I raised to $16, $18, $20, $24 and so on. I kept a chart of the number of subscribers month by month and could not see that a raise in price made the slightest dent in the consistent upward curve. I came to realize that people put no higher value on your product than you put on it yourself.

One thing I held to consistently and contrary to the practice of most publications: I kept the half-year rate at exactly half the full-year rate. I did not want to penalize the little guy. Better to bill twice a year than not have the customer at all.

As the issues tumbled out, one after another, every other Wednesday, the newsletter carried more confidence that it had found a worthwhile place. Under the heading, "How's Northwest Business?" the opening page clicked off fast answers on employment, the lumber market, department stores sales, residential construction, food processing, bank loans, per capita income — the endless bits and pieces that, put together, tell a reader what's happening in his own backyard.

The inside pages swung into more detailed analysis of what's happening industry by industry — lumber & plywood, metal-working, pulp & paper, textiles & apparel, flour milling, aluminum, consumer credit, farm income, and so on. The focus was on *what* and *why*. One issue told what's back of a bus strike. Another, what's happening at Boeing. Then, why the boom in the apparel industry.

The look was ahead. As the year 1950 opened, the letter headlined, "Big growth lies ahead for the Northwest" and spelled out five underlying factors. But just as candidly it told the "other side of the picture — the tough nuts the NW must crack." The newsletter emphasized the positive and cited ways that the regional base was expanding, as in this tiny item from an early issue:

"Getting business: Pacific Waxed Paper Co., Seattle, (A.B. Engle, W.B. Parsons) recently installed the first five-color rotogravure press on the Coast to print waxed paper overwraps for frozen food. Previously, NW packers had to go East for this work. Now the company is running three shifts on overwraps."

The newsletter had one taboo: Anything that had appeared in the daily papers was as dead as a fallen leaf. But there were times, as we shall see, when a tiny innocuous newspaper squib hardly worth notice became the starting point for a full story spread over the newsletter's middle two pages.

Work was endless. I needed subscribers and acknowledged every subscription the day it came in. I typed the envelopes for subscribers on mailing day. I continued reporting and writing without letup for *Business Week* and tradepapers. How long could I hang on? Fighting to finish a job or get stuff into that day's outgoing mail, I was so often late coming home for 6 p.m. supper that I had this arrangement with

Dot: When I'd be late, I'd phone home, let the phone ring once, then hang up. When there was only one ring, Dot knew she should call me. Because the office phone was on metered service and my home was not, I saved five cents on each call.

Of this time I remember vividly that walking home from the bus I was often so tired that all I wanted to do was lie down on the grassy parking strip. And poor Dot! For me to come home late and worn out was no way to treat such a loyal helpmate.

The response of those who subscribed — and those who didn't — was critical in shaping the letter. The first issue drew from Leith F. Abbott, head of the Portland office of Foote, Cone & Belding, a cautious come-on: "It will be interesting to see if the Pacific Northwest has reached the stage of development where a news letter of this kind can be published profitably. I hope so."

The second issue brought a stinger from Dick Lamb. That issue, he wrote, "is good but I found myself dozing over the furniture [manufacturing] story. I still think that anything of this length, no matter how good, is inconsistent with the purpose of a news letter. I felt cheated."

D.W. Walters, head of Inland Empire Industrial Research in Spokane, kindly tagged the newsletter "a very fine quick summary of current business conditions ...a good picture right here on our own home grounds."

Howard Ryan, head of a Seattle advertising agency, wrote on his order for a year: "Nicely fills an obvious need. Congrats!"

A.A. Wakefield, office manager of U. S. Steel Supply Co., Seattle, called the letter "especially helpful to us in preparing periodic reports to our Chicago office about Northwest business conditions."

Writing as a relative newcomer, Howard W. Morgan, manager of Weyerhaeuser's pulp division, ordered a subscription sent to his home: "The feature that appeals to me is the amount of news that you have about Northwest industries. We manage to keep pretty well informed about our own industry, but I doubt if any of us has anything but a very vague idea as to what goes on in the chemical, the power, or the fertilizer industry."

Subscribers were searching, too. Guy W. Conner, a Portland broker of steel products, wrote: "We will take this for six months and see if you do us any good in locating buyers and sellers for railroad steel and accessories, or anything we don't get from the Wall Street Journal and other trade journals."

Douglas B. Lewis at the San Francisco office of E.F. Hutton & Co., was "particularly interested in any news item on Pacific Coast Co., Seattle,...their several divisions in coal, oil, appliances and land."

William E. Welch, Seattle manager of Timber Structures, "sold several jobs based on leads developed by your letter." But there was no help for a Yakima Valley potato dealer who asked for "any records on contracts let for dehydrated potatoes."

L.V. Hall, Blake, Moffitt & Towne, Tacoma, was critical: "This is the third copy I have received and in these letters not one mention of Tacoma, an important industrial center of the Northwest."

As subscriptions came up for renewal, there were turndowns, too. From Phillips Dickinson at Seattle Bronze Co.: "My reason for discontinuing...there is just too much general information and not enough specific information about our particular industry, industrial and architectural aluminum and bronze fabrication."

And from Hollis Farwell, Alexander & Baldwin, Seattle: "Fine publication but no longer require it. Please cancel."

Not long after the start of the newsletter Dick McCarty, a thin, wiry advertising salesman for the monthly tradepaper *Western Advertising*, blew in on me. I had done some reporting for the magazine but mighty little because it paid so little. McCarty, working out of the San Francisco office, made sales calls in Seattle every few months. He was full of curiosity and help for what I was doing. He remarked once in writing of a forthcoming visit, "as you probably have figured, the possibilities of this newsletter business interest me exceedingly."

McCarty had some suggestions on editorial content, but his great value to me was his knowledge and enthusiasm for sales promotion. He went over in detail every sales letter and fired an endless stream of questions and ideas. What was the response to various types of trial subscription? How much difference whether the trial was for two months, three months, or a trial five issues? One evening at the office he went over the names of subscribers one by one and asked the position of each subscriber in his company. McCarty was impressed.

His were searching questions. How did the reply card read? Did colored paper or colored ink have any effect? What was the renewal rate? What was the response when I followed up with a personal note to any subscriber who did not renew? What response to questionnaires to find topics of greatest interest? He was a tonic for a one-man shop.

Quite early McCarty mentioned that one specialist in direct-mail concluded that it was a mistake to enclose the product in the sales package; when you gave the product away, the argument went, there was no reason to buy. But I countered that no one knew Marple, no one knew the newsletter, and I had to show what I was selling. McCarty checked the response I was getting and never again raised the question.

When McCarty was in town Dot suggested that I bring him home for dinner. The talk was lively but ran on so late that Dot and I between ourselves began to call him "2 a.m. McCarty."

The subscription list grew, though slowly. I bought a used Addressograph machine to address envelopes to subscribers. I continued this dependable but cumbersome addressing equipment until Mike Parks and computers came in. It was hand-operated, one envelope at a time. Its heavy clunk-clunk told anyone in an office nearby that another mailing was coming up. I had a lettershop print sales letters, reply cards, order forms and such, but it was a long time before I bought a used postage meter that did away with the licking of stamps. I drew on savings to pay the office rent and keep the landlord, Norbert Schaal, happy. His kindly draftswoman took the rare phone calls that came when I was hustling news.

Short as the subscription list still was, its breadth was encouraging — banks, public utilities, libraries, manufacturers (in lumber and paper, steel, foods, chemicals, machinery for the forest industry, consumer goods), plus wholesalers, trade associations and a few department stores. A diverse lot.

Six months into the newsletter I responded to an inquiry from Dick Lamb: "It goes along pretty well. At least I am out of the stage where it is taking money out of my pocket. But there isn't much return yet for my time. August was my best month with around 50 or 60 new subs. Now I am in the good season for direct mail and want to make the most of it.

"My problem is that of any small manufacturer: I spend so much time and energy on production that I don't have time and energy to spend on sales. But you have to produce the egg before you can peddle it. Like small mfrs. I can't pay for outside help that I know I ought to have. But it's a lot of fun!"

I was learning. A month later, having just run a very difficult two-page special report, "Power Shortage Curbs Industrial Development," I wrote Lamb: "I had more calls of comment on this issue than on any issue so far. Half a dozen persons volunteered that it was a swell job (which it was). But the new subscriptions were the poorest of any issue since the beginning, viz., 3."

Stories on electric power were the most difficult I ever did. The subject was so complex. It involved management of power dams on the Columbia River system, storage of water in Canada, a tie-line to California, and diverse demands of preference customers, aluminum mills, and big power users. The newsletter warned that "a grim shortage of electric power [would] close this region for several years to basic new industries that require lots of electric energy."

Noting to Lamb that this issue was a flop as to new orders, I concluded "my customers want constructive news and suggestions. They want an antidote to Kiplinger and the Washington boys with the tears. They want things they can apply to their business — to increase business. They want stuff they can use to prime their salesmen. They don't want to spend money for something that says: 'Sit down, bub; you're licked.' The surprising amount of interest in the short notes about company expansions, new products, and new campaigns indicates the same thing."

The style of writing was established by now. Nothing stood ahead of clarity and understanding. The ideas, the development of a topic, had to flow smoothly from the first sentence, and right to the end. Sentences were short; if possible, not more than one line. Paragraphs were short; almost never more than six lines. A page could not exceed 60 lines. When a draft, perhaps a second or third or fourth rewrite, still ran a few lines over, there was nothing to do but crank the story once more through the meat-grinder — the typewriter — and cut, rephrase and rewrite. Each word had to carry its weight, or out it went.

I often said that if I had twice the space I could write the newsletter in half the time. That's an understatement. A tag-end paragraph in an early issue emphasized that the newsletter was a condensed report: "In preparing each issue we gather enough material to fill 8 to 10 newsletters. This is summarized to save your time. For additional detail on any subject, call or write us." Yes, I did now and then get a call, and I'd knock out a three or four page elaboration in far less time than it took to write the original condensed item.

Every other Monday was go-to-press day, a day of final rewriting, of putting the results of legwork, interviews, correspondence and analysis into meaningful form. It was always a hard day. When I came to work that morning I had to have before me a draft in rough form.

By the end of the day I had to turn that draft into four pages of clean-typed camera-ready copy to stick under the door of the printer in his little shop just beyond the Pike Place Market. The printer, Herm Jondal, knew he could start work on my job Tuesday morning and deliver the newsletters for mailing that afternoon.

My father, Lucius E. Marple, then past 80, came in Monday to "read copy." A retired businessman, he was an excellent grammarian who years earlier had taught English at a prestigious Boston prep school. He questioned as he read: "Why do you say it this way? It's not clear." Or, "What are you really trying to say?" Or, "Wouldn't it be simpler to turn that paragraph around?" He also pointed out something that I had not learned in all my schooling and newspaper work: "The beginning and the end of a sentence are the strong parts; write to that emphasis." Whatever reputation the newsletter gained for terseness and directness I owe to my father. And there was always, of course, the unrelenting challenge of a newsletter — so much to say and to say gracefully in such short space.

I always figured that some among my readers knew next to nothing about a topic I'd be writing about, and some others knew more than I'd ever know. I had to be clear to the first group and yet provide useful information or perspective to the second group — all without a stumble that revealed my ignorance. The ultimate compliment came after an interview on a complex topic: "That man understood what I was talking about."

I was slow to realize that it was not enough to carry news that was important. The reader has to recognize its importance. One way is to add perspective. Eileen Shanahan, skillful business writer on *The New York Times*, once remarked that a single figure standing alone means nothing; there must be a second figure for comparison. If you cite the current unemployment rate, she would say, you need to compare that with unemployment in an earlier significant period, or throw in a percentage change. She was adding perspective though she did not call it that.

McFadden in San Francisco was a great help in punching up the importance of what I was reporting. In the first year of the newsletter he wrote that he was "flattered on being asked about your editorial slants. I have felt it could be better dramatized but hesitated to say so since I recognize that one person's style is not applicable everywhere."

Then he picked some examples from one issue: "For immediate (soft talk) you might say, right off the bat." Of lumber, then the region's largest industry, say: "Lumber, the No. 1 pocket book filler in the NW." Later he came up with "lumber, as important to the NW as oil to Texas." To my item on pulp mills, he would add, "a high volume, close margin business at the best." He would broaden an item about Northwest mine officials with the phrase, "always touchy over imports." He explained: "I always try to stick in some background information to make it more informative and also give the impression that I know a hell of a lot more than I am telling and maybe I will shoot everything in the next issue."

Another time he wrote: "Your stuff shows excellent substance but I think it might stand a little more showmanship." As a suggestion he cited pet expressions he sometimes used in his own newsletters: "Outstanding development of the week." Or "of Grade A long-range importance, only slightly less for shorter term." And, a bit plushier: "An obscure development only partially recognized and even less understood, may in coming months turn out to be the top news of the year." He acknowledged that this was "sort of cheap soap boxing, but you will be surprised how damn many things turn into 'sensational developments.'" I got his point.

Beyond a matter of style I set some simple office rules. I answered mail the day it came in. If I didn't, there had to be a good reason. I wrote an individual note of thanks for every new subscription the day it came in, and I tucked in with the note the requested back issues from the list we offered. I was intent on distinguishing this little business from national publications that took subscriptions with the caveat, "allow four weeks for fulfillment."

I paid bills the day they arrived. It cost no more to pay today than 30 days later, and that prompt check bought a lot of good will — and sometimes service I could not ask for. When the telephone rang, I answered it, even after I had a secretary. None of this, "Who's calling, please? I'll see if he is in."

For several years until I had a secretary I took the newsletter for the final camera-ready typing to Ethel Shelton, a wisp of a fiery woman who ran a letter shop (a small printshop) in the Northern Life Tower. She had no trouble reading the goose tracks of my final editing. But when she was on vacation I nearly died typing on her electric typewriter a letter-perfect final copy for the bigger press that the newsletter required. My own typing, from early newspaper days, was based on speed, easily corrected by pencil on a page of goose tracks.

Ethel also printed my sales letters, order forms, renewal notices and the like. Her work was fast, neat and dependable. She did a lot of printing for lawyers in the building and liked to work with customers whose needs she understood. But don't cross her! Well along in life she married Lloyd Edwards, a widower. They were a delightful couple. But never send anything, not even a Christmas card, addressed to Mrs. Lloyd Edwards. She remained to the end Ethel Shelton. In time the computer made print-shops such as hers obsolete and she returned to her native Walla Walla to finish out her days.

My brother Warren, economist and department head at Bonneville Power Administration, Portland, more than once expressed surprise that as only one person I got so much done, issue after issue of the newsletter.

The answer was simple: There was no staff meeting to eat up time. There were no anguished memos to the boss or endless requests for somebody down the line to review and respond. There were no office politics that churn the stomach and break one's sleep. There was no coffee break or chit-chat at the water cooler; indeed, no water cooler and no coffee pot; just productive work and the goad that when a self-employed person stops working, the pay stops and the next deadline looms larger. If an idea looked good, go ahead and do it. If it flopped, drop it and get on with something else. The game was fun.

Chapter Four
The Push for Subscribers

The subscription list built slowly and, it seemed, almost grudgingly. As a bit of cheer McFadden suggested that when the first $2 introductory subscriptions expired they would be replaced with renewals at the annual rate and thus begin to bring in some dollars. Maybe.

By the end of the first year I had 177 subscribers. A year later, 420. I figured that if I got to 1,000 I could hang on forever. I little realized that it would take nearly eight years to reach that level and almost 20 years more to reach my top of 3,400 when Mike Parks came in.

When people asked how the newsletter was going, I had a simple answer: "Not badly enough to kill, not well enough to talk about." Roughly one-third of net income came from the newsletter, one-third from *Business Week*, and one-third from tradepapers. As the newsletter grew, I dropped the poorer-paying tradepapers.

Even the concept of a regional business letter was new and had to be sold. Promotion centered on the samples that went out every issue with a sales letter, generally a one-page typewritten sheet, nothing fancy, no four-color brochure on glossy paper.

As one way to become known I mailed free to a list from West Coast Fast Freight, a truck line operating throughout the Pacific Northwest. The list included names and addresses of 700 customers, station managers and freight solicitors. I mailed eight issues with the compliments of West Coast Fast Freight, then followed with a low-pressure sales pitch. I don't recall that it produced many new customers and I did not expect it would. But the exposure was good when the newsletter was just starting, the printing of extra copies was cheap, and so was postage at three cents for first-class mail.

Early on when the newsletter was struggling to find its place, I dropped a note to several subscribers asking for a few words that I could use with their name for promotion. Several replied, generously, and I printed a sheet of responses that I tucked in with sales mail and occasionally with a renewal notice.

One customer declined, "very loathe," he wrote, "to give written recommendations for any venture." But he went on with the very helpful suggestion of what he wanted to find in the newsletter. The writer was William S. Street, president of Frederick & Nelson, one of the great department stores of America. (Many years after his retirement the store, under new ownership and management, stumbled into bankruptcy and oblivion.)

Mr. Street explained why he turned me down. "At the announcement of your new publication," he wrote, "we subscribed in order that we might help you in this business venture and at the same time with the expectation we would acquire some knowledge of the Pacific Northwest area....

"My idea of a letter of this sort fundamentally is one that deals with facts. We are not interested in gossipy predictions. If you take a flier at that some time it is all right with us, but we hope you will continue to report as much factual matter about the Pacific Northwest as you can."

Thank you, Mr. Street! That perspective was worth far more to me than a testimonial. His letter became pinned to my mind and strengthened my purpose: to help managers see and understand better what's happening in their own front yard.

The loyalty of readers was an immense plus. Over the years our own subscribers brought in countless new subscribers. Sometimes when an order came over the transom, that is, unsolicited, the new customer mentioned that so-and-so had recommended the letter. More often, subscribers themselves introduced us directly to new readers. Once or twice a year the newsletter included a note to subscribers to the effect: "Send us the names of your customers, suppliers, associates or others and we'll mail the newsletter to them with your compliments for three months." The offer, begun many years ago, continues to the present, especially well received at Christmas time. It always brings us new subscribers, and it spreads good will among older ones.

Comments from subscribers are always helpful. Sometimes they are just a few words jotted down on a renewal, and sometimes a letter asking for extra copies that a customer found especially pertinent. Does the customer want an extra three or four extra copies, or maybe eight or ten? Glad to supply; no charge. This newsletter is a business tool, the more useful the better.

Whatever the form — a hasty note or a formal letter — the reaction of customers in time filled three overflowing file folders. Whenever I had to write yet another sales letter, I'd dig through recent comments. They served as a guide, too, for the editorial content of the newsletter itself.

Typical of the way customers passed the word, R. W. Stuart, head of Sumner Iron Works, Everett, wrote: "If the following [four companies] are not subscribers, I would appreciate your sending them a copy of your October 10, 1951, issue, marking the section headed 'Pushing Back the Barriers,' with my compliments."

Helen B. Sawyers, Credit Bureau of Snohomish County, Everett, sent a quick note: "May I pass along the name of a prospective subscriber? [He] is new to our area and is a Kiplinger fan. Your letter is so much more factual and valuable for the Northwest that I know he will want it."

As time went on the newsletter picked up a smattering of subscriptions from a distance — flattering but not significant in revenue. G.B. MacKenzie in the economic analysis section of Ford Motor in Dearborn, Michigan, reported "the information we get in the Business Roundup, fortnightly, is so useful to us" that he asked if we knew of "publications of a similar nature for other sections of the nation." Sorry, no.

The Federal Reserve Bank of San Francisco was an early and devoted subscriber. Harry S. Schwartz, head of research, wrote January 27, 1955: "Your Business Roundup contributes a great deal to our assessment of the situation in the Pacific Northwest....The qualitative conditions surrounding changes in business are frequently as important as the changes themselves, since they may be forerunners of attitudes and expectations that have not yet been revealed."

Sometimes, also, there was a thorn in the mail. "Discontinue," Salmon Bay Sand & Gravel Co., Seattle, jotted on its renewal notice; "interesting but not pertinent to our business." Another subscriber scrawled "cancel" on the renewal notice and growled: "You don't know any more than we do."

One of the great fans of the newsletter was Miner H. Baker, economist and vice-president of Seafirst Bank. When the newsletter was in its second year Miner Baker asked how much I'd charge for a subscription for a dozen or so top officers and all branch managers. Miner related long afterward that some bank officers had come to him to suggest that he duplicate the newsletter and distribute it within the bank. "No," Miner said, "that's not fair to Elliot." Instead he suggested a group subscription at a reduced rate, a source of income I had never thought of.

I got out my pencil and tried to figure a rate so low that the bank could not pass it up. My additional cost would be slight, mainly postage and envelopes. I came back with a price of $3 a year for each copy, less than a quarter of the single subscription. "You won't make money on that," Miner responded, so we settled on $5 a year for each of 45 copies in a single order.

Subsequently I boosted the price as the rate for a single subscription rose, and the bank added more names as it acquired new branches and more officers at the Seattle headquarters. In time the total expanded to 321 copies; (with mergers and branch closings the number dropped in 1999 to 50. To eliminate the cost of postage and envelopes I took a bundle of copies on mailing day to the bank's central mailing room and let it handle distribution.

Later a similar arrangement was worked out with the next largest statewide bank, National Bank of Commerce, and with several much smaller banks and savings & loan associations. One bank, long since lost in merger, had a dozen branches in small outlying cities. It was easy to see how the letter might help the manager of the only bank in town keep perspective as he looked out to a drab, unchanging Main Street. One such town, Winlock, lay alongside the main line of the railroad between Seattle and Portland, miles from any freeway. Just outside the Winlock train station stood a mammoth painted egg, perhaps eight feet high, the proud symbol of the town's business — eggs and poultry.

Bulk subscriptions carried a plus for the newsletter. There was nothing like having a loan officer ask a customer: "Did you see what Marple said in the current issue?"

Miner Baker's Quarterly Review ranked among the best bank publications in the nation. Miner was articulate as writer and speaker and in constant demand before business and civic audiences. After Miner's retirement, Mike Parks, articulate likewise, took on speaking assignments throughout the Pacific Northwest and in time became, in effect, Miner's successor as spokesman on the economy.

Early in development of the bank's quarterly publication, Miner surprised me by asking me to join him. He had cleared with bank management the position, the salary, and the title of assistant vice-president, a strong come-on for a young outsider. The salary was more than I was then earning. It was tempting. But I had worked so hard to get as far as I had on the newsletter that I was not ready to give up. Besides, I relished my independence and the ability to start each morning doing what I thought was most important that day, and if

Howard Staples, - 1952

Marple gets the news; on-the-spot interview with George Burwell, Ace Tank & Equipment Co.

things went awry, there was only myself to blame. So for Miner it was: no, thanks!

Many years later Miner in retirement recalled the incident and wrote: "We would have been a formidable team — but each too good in his own right (I like to think) to generate that extra force that comes from team play. I may not have said that well. The point is that you made the right decision — although I also made the right one in approaching you."

Miner and I toiled in the same field — the Pacific Northwest economy — but with quite different publications. Miner's Quarterly Review was scholarly and delightfully presented. It was a rich resource that included analysis, forecast and the finest compilation of regional statistics. Sometimes we overlapped. The newsletter had the advantage of brevity, flexibility and frequency of issue. One day Miner wrote:

"I hate you! I have just finished reading your October 5 issue, and it leaves me wondering what there is left to say about Boeing in the upcoming issue of our Quarterly Review....You're just too damned good." He signed it "grudgingly" — a compliment certain to buck up a fellow working alone.

Jumping ahead a few years I might interject that that was not the last job offer growing out of the newsletter. An inquiry in more general terms came from W.L. (Wigs) Campbell, after he became president of Safeco Corp. He and I had met earlier when he was a young officer. We were on an out-of-town industrial tour and had a long, far-roaming conversation on the way to Grays Harbor. But again it was no, thanks! The newsletter by this time had become better established, and I had worked alone so long and so strenuously that I figured I had become occupationally disqualified to work for anyone else.

The newsletter was not three years old when it got an unexpected break — a feature story in *Business Week* headlined: "Man-at-a-Typewriter Journalism."

The story centered on three newsletters—*Kiplinger* for a national newsletter, *Petty Washington Newsletter* for an industry letter, and *Marple's* for an independent regional letter. The illustration was all Marple—three photographs of the man at work, in the office and out on an interview. As the magazine told it:

> "*Marple's Business Roundup* is a good example of the general-interest regional newsletters. A typical issue follows this pattern of content:
>
> "A quick front-page review of Northwest business conditions. Statistics are cited, but only as the peg for an explanation of what they mean. Example: A few months ago, savings deposits were running behind the previous year while Portland's were up $15-million. Marple interviewed bankers and dug out the reasons.
>
> "A full-dress report on a major industry or a tough regional problem.
>
> "A series of short paragraphs about specific companies, industries, areas, markets, products. No gossip, though.
>
> "Tricky Slant — Marple in his own region has the same problem as Kiplinger and Whaley-Eaton in their nationwide field: to interest subscribers in subjects that aren't directly related to their various businesses.
>
> "'In effect,' says Marple, 'I'm selling a reader a general education on Northwest business and industry. There's no question that if the Roundup were confined in subject to the particular industry or trade of the subscriber it would be easier to prove that it's a necessary tool in his business.'
>
> "Marple meets this problem as any general-interest magazine meets it: He keeps a deft balance between variety and depth, between a wide range of topics and sufficient detail to give a reader the background of an unfamiliar subject."

That story, like almost everything in the magazine, was written in New York. Dick Lamb in the San Francisco bureau certainly had a hand in it. I submitted to him a memo and answers to a long string of questions. One of his questions: "Could you include a paragraph or two along the lines of our earlier discussion that the regional newsletter business is far from a gold mine? If I were reporting this story I would say that the fuel that keeps MBR [the Roundup] going is your own (Scottish?) cussedness, your determination to keep it alive — not because it's the only way you can feed four hungry mouths but because you're too bullheaded to let it die. I would also put in something about how much time you spend on this and your other revenue-producing labors — how many hours per week on the average."

The story had a rare twist. I got paid space rates for writing about myself. I don't remember how much, but the check sure came as a happy surprise.

Howard Staples, - 1952
Elliot Marple taps out the next issue in his Bay Building office

Chapter Five
Business Week

*B*usiness Week was not only generous in writing about the newsletter; it was also the most important customer of my one-man news bureau. I could not have carried through the early years without it. In some months I earned as much from this magazine as from all the tradepapers combined. In addition, its assignments for news sent me ranging throughout the Pacific Northwest. Beyond this, I had the stimulus and fun of working with excellent editors, notably Richard J. Lamb Jr. in San Francisco; Edgar A. Grunwald, managing editor, responsible for the product that went to subscribers and newsstands every Friday; and Robert Colborn, gifted editor and writer, remarkable for his search for new ideas.

Seattle, Portland and the rest of the Pacific Northwest were growing in national importance, and as Lamb often remarked, the magazine took from me a disproportionate volume of news. This was some years before Microsoft, Nike, Starbucks, Nordstrom, Paccar, Safeco and Washington Mutual became known nationwide. It was before the regional timber companies — Weyerhaeuser, Georgia-Pacific, Boise Cascade and Willamette Industries — spread into the South, before the ports on Puget Sound and the Columbia River grew large with container trade across the Pacific, and even before Boeing became a name heard the world over.

I first met Ed Grunwald in Washington, D.C., when he was a thoughtful, careful young reporter covering the war agencies. I met Lamb later when I was opening shop in Seattle and Lamb cautiously watched to see who this guy Marple was and what if any use he might be. As the working relationship developed, I felt like an equal in passing along ideas for stories beyond my area and occasional suggestions that might help the New York editors take some of the bumps out of the management of a national magazine.

I was proud of this connection, and my business card, down in the left corner, read: "Correspondent for Business Week." I think that the magazine had a clearer field than in today's stiff competition.

"One of the things that surprised me when I started covering for *BW*," I wrote Lamb in 1951, "and one of the things that clearly is its strength is its freedom from the sort of bias you might expect from a publication written for businessmen. I was interested to find labor men, e.g., reading *BW* and speaking warmly of its coverage, particularly of labor."

Lamb and Grunwald were generous in their comment. In response to a story-memo that I sent directly to New York as part of a nationwide survey, Lamb wrote: "That was a thoughtful, thorough job you did on taxes, working capital, etc. Should be very heartening to the guy [in New York] who has to pull the story together."

A little later Lamb wrote of his carbon copy of a forest products story that I had sent directly to New York: "I haven't seen the pix, of course, but I have read the text of your memo on forest products. And as usual I think you have done a superlative job. I say this at risk of inviting your wrath for my failure to criticize. On second thought, though, I can criticize: You misspelled Pope & Talbot on p13. Fie on you."

One day after an exchange about my compensation, I tossed off a quick comment: "I appreciate your note about compensation and your thoughtfulness. I certainly don't want to become anyone's problem-child." Lamb returned the note with this penned comment: "Oh Lord, if I could only have a nursery full of such problem-children!" To my other comment, "nor do I expect any better treatment than I earn," Lamb added generously: "That's just the point. Measured by conventional standards, you earn a hell of a lot better treatment than our needs in Seattle warrant our paying. But the luxury of having a guy like you to work with, in Seattle or Peoria, is well worth paying for, in my view."

Grunwald was always warm. The Bugle, his monthly report to some 30 part-time correspondents, set out the honey of cash awards, generally $20 to $25 [multiply by about eight to equal 1999 dollars]. One month Grunwald listed: "Elliot Marple, (freelance, Seattle) $35. For writing memos on his area that are meaty, complete, intelligent. Great guy, this Marple — always a prize-winner."

A year later: "Elliot Marple (freelance) Seattle: $50. Dick Lamb suggested this one, and I'm sweetening the pot a bit because Marple consistently does what we want all of you to do all the time — he sparks ideas. Think, men, think. It will pay off. This is Marple's fifth Bugle prize and sets a record."

Technically, I was just a stringer, an unsalaried reporter paid space rates for each job done and for anything ordered but not used. The term stringer originated many years ago among country weeklies when a part-timer writing about local events pasted up and sent in a string of clippings to which an editor took a ruler and paid by the inch. The term "stringer" has largely given way to "correspondent."

I never knew or worried how much I might get for an assignment on a major story — for the research and writing and for helping a skilled photographer provide illustration on 35-millimeter film. Compensation became more generous as time ran on, and *Business Week* in the early years put me on a monthly guarantee that I usually exceeded. Later it tossed in a monthly fee for attending such events as a news conference where the magazine wanted to be represented even though nothing newsworthy might develop.

Business Week maintained news bureaus in more than a dozen cities around the country, each staffed by one or several full-time salaried reporters. For many years its only West Coast bureaus were in San Francisco and Los Angeles. It had stringers in Portland, Seattle and at various times Spokane, Boise and Salt Lake City, all under Lamb's supervision. Stringers in small cities often lost interest; their work for the magazine was such a small part of their total income, and they were often baffled by how the New York office operated or what its highly specialized department editors wanted.

Each summer *Business Week* brought its entire U. S. staff — from New York and all the bureaus — to a three-day seminar in an eastern resort, away from the distractions of New York. I was one of only two stringers invited to a gathering in the Pocono Mountains of Pennsylvania in 1976, an opportunity to meet editors known previously only by mail or phone and to sit in on talks by eminent outsiders. Flattering!

The magazine did not yet need a full-time bureau in Seattle, but I tried to give it the coverage, attention and speedy handling of just such a bureau. Mike Parks as my successor continued this responsibility until the growth of the newsletter squeezed him for time, and the emergence of the Puget Sound computer industry warranted the magazine's opening its first Seattle bureau in 1994. Easy air travel also enables a magazine to fly in specialized reporters from San Francisco and Los Angeles.

Together, Marple and Parks provided more than 40 years of news coverage for *Business Week*.

Chapter Six
What is News?

"How do you get your news?" was a common question. The simplest answer: By asking questions, and the most important question is *why*.

For example, a government agency releases a figure on current employment. The raw figure means nothing. So you start by putting with it another figure such as employment a month ago, or a year ago, or in a recent forecast. Thus alerted, you then ask yourself, Why the change? What's happening in the economy? As you dig you may turn to a breakdown of employment by industry and trade and ask, where specifically is the change coming from? You also talk to someone who can answer the *why* within a particular industry. All along you look for a trend, a pattern that may help in the look ahead. In this instance the tell-tale is not the *what* (the raw figure) but the *why*.

Sometimes you look beyond the company to what others in the same industry are doing. When QFC, then an independent supermarket chain, released its quarterly report on sales and earnings, you divide earnings by sales and find that it earned a nickel on each dollar of sales. Five percent sounds low, and by comparison with manufacturers in electronics the return is piddling. But nationwide, supermarkets do well to average just over one percent — a penny earned on each dollar of sales. Now you look again at QFC, and you say Wow! How did they make 5%? [In the last couple of years the national average has edged up, and QFC's cost in opening new stores pulled its phenomenal return down a bit. Recently QFC was acquired by Fred Meyer, and Fred Meyer by Kroger.]

Again the question: Where do you get the news? My reporting for other business papers was sometimes a great help, especially in the early days. McFadden's *Western Packing News Service*, for example, covered food canning and freezing. If there were new companies or mergers of food companies in the Pacific Northwest, he wanted to know, fast. Each June I had to keep him posted on the outlook for frozen peas in the Blue Mountain area around Walla Walla. The immense output of that area, scarcely recognized in Seattle or Portland, affected prices nationwide.

McFadden published two issues a month of each of his papers and wanted from me at least once a month a profile of a food packer. Thus I came to know the companies and people in this industry, so basic to the Pacific Northwest economy, and I always looked for carry-over to my newsletter.

There was a similar interplay of news about the Alaska salmon industry that in big years packed as many as 12-million cases, 48 one-pound cans to the case. McFadden wanted to know what was going on in salmon. So did *Food Field Reporter* in New York and sometimes *Business Week*. The industry was too production-minded to get together on promotion, but New England Fish Co. of Seattle, the one consistent national advertiser of canned salmon, always made news for me for *Advertising Age*. New England Fish Co., which did indeed come out of New England, has since disappeared from business, and the industry has changed. Salmon, instead of going to market in cans, now goes mostly fresh or frozen. Loaded into the bellies of jet aircraft, the fish reach markets in Europe and Japan overnight.

Produce News, the smaller of two national weekly newspapers for the fresh fruit and vegetable industry and known as the "pink sheet" from the color of its paper, didn't have space for much news week by week. But once a year it really came alive with a fat issue for the industry's national convention. For this it gobbled up all the news I could send. I hopped in the car to spend a couple of days talking with shippers and packers up and down the Yakima Valley and in Wenatchee. The Pink Sheet's pay was poor at a penny a word but the stories were easy to write and ran long. Most important, they gave me insight on another part of the Pacific Northwest economy.

Chapter Seven
The Changing Forest Industry

Some of the best stories came out of savvy built up bit by bit — an understanding of the economy and some of its players. This spotting of the significant distinguishes a newsletter from daily papers with their concentration on what happens to pop up new each day.

One Saturday I came to work with the usual Saturday thermos of coffee and a sandwich, prepared to finish by that night a rough draft of the next issue. I had done all the reporting, but at breakfast I spotted a tiny item in the morning paper that announced the merger of two old-line lumber companies — Boise Payette in Boise and Cascade in Yakima. Just a couple of sentences, routine.

But wait a minute! Something bigger must be cooking. These were two conservative manufacturers in an industry where margins were tightening, the cost of raw material was rising, and big producers were integrating vertically — from lumber into pulp and paper. Couldn't the sawmills of these two companies together produce enough slabs, edgings and other mill waste to support a new pulp mill?

One fact glared at me: Robert V. Hansberger, the new president of Boise Payette, was fresh out of the pulp and paper industry. He had been schooled at Container Corporation of America in Chicago, then built and ran the pulp mill of Western Kraft Corp. in Albany, Oregon, the first pulp mill in the Pacific Northwest to operate solely on the wood waste of lumber mills.

I spent long-distance phone money very charily, but that morning I hopped fast on the phone to Boise, hoping, as indeed I found, that a man with big plans would be at his desk on Saturday. Hansberger knew me. I did not expect him to cut loose with his plans, but I needed to verify the big story that I read into that little item in the morning paper. He knew I would not pin him down with quotes, and he readily answered my questions: Yes, a pulp mill would be logical in the merger. Yes, the likely place for such a mill would be on the Columbia River below Pasco. Yes, the two companies owned enough forest land to assure a long-time supply of raw material, 428,000 acres, one of the larger holdings in the Pacific Northwest. And yes to several other surmises. The pieces fit.

I had my story for the middle two pages of the next issue: an example of how Pacific Northwest lumber companies were merging so as to diversify into pulp & paper and reach out nationwide. This merger, the newsletter said, "will rank Boise Cascade as one of the largest lumber producers in the West. Yet lumber is not the focus of the merger. The one underlying purpose is to provide an adequate base for more complete utilization of forest resources. Together the two companies will be able to do what neither can do alone in processing by-products and thus in recovering additional values from every tree. The merged company can afford necessary research and build new plants such as for pulp & paper, particle board, hardboard, plywood, etc., with the assurance of enough raw material to warrant the investment.

"This trend was summed up by one old-timer: 'You cannot make money in a sawmill today just by cutting lumber. Your profit must come from using every stick from the forest, and every bit of mill waste.' This simple fact is reshaping the entire industry and is giving the Pacific NW new growth and diversity in manufacturing.

"But there's a catch: the processing of mill by-products requires substantial investment. A pulp plant cannot be justified unless back of it are large timber reserves for sustained operation."

A bit farther along the story became specific: "It would be no surprise to see a pulp mill on the Columbia River below Pasco, a crossroads for rail and water transportation and a central point for Boise Cascade."

Thus began Boise Cascade Corp. It indeed built its first pulp mill on the Columbia, just below Pasco at Wallula. It expanded in the West and later added lumber and paper mills in the South, where cheaper timber and a shorter haul to market give an unbeatable edge. Today Boise Cascade's sales exceed $6 billion a year. It has 20,000 stockholders and nearly that many employees — the giant that grew from the merger of two lumber manufacturers too small to go it alone.

The "old-timer" quoted but not identified in the above report on Boise Cascade was Ralph Brown, a retired lumberman. He was of immense help to me in understanding the evolving forest industry. Because I wanted him to speak freely and he wanted no personal attention, I never quoted him by name.

For a balance in reporting I also looked in on the regional managers of the two separate unions for lumber and plywood, one AFL, the other CIO. I found these men open and helpful though their rivalry ran so deep that they would not talk to each other — until merger came from on top. I also kept in touch with the long-time business representative in Seattle of the pulp and paper union, Oren Parker. He was exceptionally well informed and in retirement remains a great fan of the newsletter.

Mr. Brown — I always called him Mr. — was perhaps 70, portly and delightfully unhurried. He held down the Seattle office of West Coast Lumbermen's Association, which represented mills in the Douglas fir area (west of the Cascade crest). When the center of the lumber industry shifted to Oregon, the association took its offices to Portland, where it served as spokesman and lobbyist for the largest group of lumber producers in the nation and gathered weekly statistics on production and sales.

When the association moved to Portland, Mr. Brown said no, he would remain in Seattle. He kept the office in the White-Henry-Stuart Building (later torn down and replaced by the Rainier Square shopping mall and office tower). White-Henry-Stuart, a prestige address, housed a number of lumber brokers. Sometimes I stuck my head in on them on a Saturday morning for a last-minute check on the lumber market. The five-day week was not yet universal. Brokers who sent "rollers" (unsold carloads) east could hardly take a day off. With a close eye to the market, a broker would buy a carload of lumber from a mill, send the car east and then, before the car reached a Midwest transfer point, have to find a wholesale yard or a builder to buy that particular assortment of sizes and grades.

Mr. Brown had wrapped his life in lumber. I found him a rich source of information. Now and again I dropped in on him when something turned up that made me want to ask *why*. One morning I came to him with a newspaper clipping on a plan to build a $35 million pulp mill on Grays Harbor, near Aberdeen. Was this realistic? Anne Nordstrom (not of the retailing family), Mr. Brown's long-time secretary, ushered me in. I stood by his desk as I spoke because I did not want to intrude; if I had come at a busy time I'd leave quickly.

"Sit down, young man," Mr. Brown admonished. "Are you in a hurry?" Sit down I did, and for more than an hour this man spilled out lessons of a lifetime, teacher to pupil.

The pulp mill announced in the newspaper, he said, would never be built (and it wasn't). You can't build one today for $35 million, he explained, and you can't borrow to build if you don't have timberland to support the mill.

Then Mr. Brown reached back in his mind to changes in this most basic of the region's industries. Each year on his drive to winter in California he poked along, visiting mills and mill operators whom he knew so well. The huge wigwam burner that once stood outside every sawmill was gone. The disappearance, Mr. Brown recalled, was a symbol of change overtaking the forest industry.

The wigwam burner, pouring out sparks, fire and acrid smoke, day and night, was once the mark of sawmill country. The burner, built of sheet steel in the shape of an Indian wigwam, stood as tall as a farm silo and devoured an endless stream of slabs, edgings, bark, and sawdust — mill waste.

But times were changing. That waste became raw material for pulp, the essential ingredient of paper. For this, the sawmill installs a barker to skin from a log the bark that a pulp mill can't digest. Then the mill slices off thin slabs to convert a round log into a square for cutting into lumber. The bark-free slabs in turn go through a chipper to become the raw material for a pulp mill.

The squeeze of economics brought big changes in the woods, too, Mr. Brown recounted. In earlier days lumber was so cheap and logs so plentiful that you couldn't afford to bring out of the forest anything but the best of logs. Now, however, wood is so valuable that you bring out low-grade logs that might otherwise go up in the smoke of a forest fire.

Mr. Brown made another point. Sawmills, once labor-intensive, have become capital-intensive. In earlier times when lumber prices tumbled, a sawmill would shut down. When the mill was ready to reopen, the manager could go down the back roads and pick up a crew of no particular skills and be cutting logs again. But now to squeeze dollars out of the ever more costly logs, a mill had to have better machinery — more precise, cutting finer, wasting less, and saving labor.

As early as 1957, Charles Young, the Weyerhaeuser economist, said in an interview for *Business Week*: "The time has passed when a sawmill could burn its waste. Chips may be the difference between profit and loss for the entire operation. But the recovery from waste may take more capital than a little fellow may have."

That trend continues. Sawmills spend heavily for computer controls and automation. They cut a log not to what the manager thinks would give him the best-looking 2x4s or 2x10s but to the sizes and grades the market wants that day.

Since Mr. Brown's time the environmental movement has brought to the forest industry a dimension that early loggers never dreamed of. The transition began, perhaps, with the leisure of long weekends. Few people today remember when the six-day week was the rule and Sunday was a day to recover. Now with long weekends, an assured vacation, and the financial means to get away, vastly more people have come to love and partake of the richness of the outdoors. To help them, to urge them on, a leisure industry has grown up — new parks and camp sites, boats on trailers to reach enticing shores, featherweight tents for back-packers, sturdy boots for mountain climbers, mountain bikes, trail maps and guides. There is no end. Automobile builders joined the outdoor world with vans for family outings and tough four-wheel drives.

Meantime research brings better handling of forests — a re-examination of harvest practice, quick replanting with improved stock, and sensitive treatment of streams and slopes. Recreation has become a force in forest management, and treasured areas are set aside in perpetual wilderness.

The transition in concepts, goals and use of the woods is the greatest change in this industry in the four centuries since New England settlers first converted massive pine forests into farmlands. A new balance in forests of the West will take time to work out. It may not come for another generation.

Chapter Eight
S. D. McFadden

Samuel D. McFadden, the San Francisco newsletter publisher whom I saw face to face only three times in my life, had greater influence than any other person in shaping the newsletter and keeping me going through the discouraging early years. He published two newsletters on the first and fifteenth of each month, *Western Packing News* for packers of canned, dried, frozen and preserved foods, and *Western Trucking News* for over-the-highway freight haulers. He was reporter, editor, sales manager and office boy. I could only marvel at how he kept up the pace year after year.

McFadden's office looms in memory dark and austere as I think back to the first time I met him. In the 25 years we worked together that was the only time I was in his office. I had heard about him in New York. In turn, he started me on a trial basis as his lookout in the Pacific Northwest. I quickly found that his two publications had an extraordinary following. Later when I launched my own newsletter and was bumping bottom, he, with the understanding of one who had traveled that road, bolstered me as no one else could.

Packing and *Trucking*, as McFadden called his publications, each looked like a cross between a newsletter and a magazine. The news was typed on letter-size sheets, three columns wide, five or six sheets to an issue. One column of the front page and sometimes inside pages carried advertising. Interleaved between the news sheets were bright page-sized ads on glossy paper such as you would see in a magazine. The format was McFadden's own.

The subscription for *Packing* was $10 a year, for *Trucking*, $7.50. Advertising from suppliers to the industry sweetened the deal. Occasionally he inserted a full-page advertisement for himself. Here was one, all in bold capital letters, brief and with lots of white space:

S. D. McFADDEN NEWS BUREAU   EXbrook 2-5235   EST 1939

Publishers of western business and industrial news services.

7 FRONT STREET
SAN FRANCISCO 11
CALIFORNIA

**WESTERN PACKING NEWS SERVICE SINCE 1939
HAS CONCENTRATED ON TWO FEATURES—**

▶ **IT CARRIES THE LIVEST NEWS
    IN THE INDUSTRY**

▶ **IT OFFERS THE LOWEST AD PRICES
    IN THE FIELD**

**MAYBE ONE, OR BOTH OF THE ABOVE IS JUST
WHAT YOUR BUSINESS NEEDS.**

I quickly saw the respect that McFadden had earned from subscribers. In my first call as a reporter for *Trucking* I walked over to Black Ball Freight Line to talk to Bob Acheson, president and owner. I was embarrassed to find myself ill-prepared; I did not yet have a business card and I forgot to bring along a copy of *Trucking*. As I fumbled to identify the newsletter, Acheson broke in: "Wait a moment, I'll get a copy" and disappeared in the bullpen of his freight-rate clerks and solicitors. He came back empty-handed. "That's typical," he grunted; "that is the only publication that comes in the office of which I read every word. When I get through I put it out for the other fellows to read, and someone has gone off with it." Acheson, a self-made man out of the prairies of Alberta, became one of my warmest news sources.

Packing carried similar respect. I passed back to McFadden this word: "You sure have a firm hold on some of the boys I talk to here. E.g., Toothman of NW Cold Pack yesterday asked who wrote your packing letter. I told him. He said whoever does sure knows his stuff and must have damn good contacts. Coddington of C.A Wilson [food] brokers, said much the same the other day — 'best letter that comes into this office; the guy who writes that sure calls his shots, digs down and knows what's going on.'"

McFadden got around. He knew the men and women in these two quite disparate industries and understood their concerns. Several years after his death I asked his wife Eleanor about this. "Yes," she said, "he got to know so many people in the field, personally. He went out in the field a great deal to call on these people. He had good leads, good tips." And he respected his sources.

As soon as McFadden picked my first issue out of his mail, he hopped on the phone: "A damn nice job." He just wanted to call up to say so because he knew that when a fellow put out his first issue he wondered why the hell he ever got in the racket.

He followed up that day with a letter of suggestions and encouragement: "Your terse, sort of clipped speech deal I think is swell....Name is nice and I think I detect some of the MCF [McFadden] angles." But he wanted to see more names, a minimum of 30 an issue [which I never was able to do].

"Think you might profitably run in a background slant with many news items. For instance...in furniture that is the industry that in twenty five years has come into being in response to westerner hopes that they could process western raw material locally....

"Glad you started it. There is nothing like having your own sheet. While the rush to try to get in dough before you run out of money isnt pleasant while in process, it is nice to look back on. Luck and it's nice to know a guy who has the guts to lay his own dough on the line without govt subsidy, etc and shoot the works."

McFadden was 38 when he founded *Packing*. He had been on *The Wall Street Journal*. As best I understood from Eleanor, he was the whole San Francisco staff in early days of that paper. He was a reporter, but he also sold subscriptions and perhaps even the installation of news tickers that were the heart of every brokerage office. He became a friend of A.P. Giannini, founder of Bank of America, and one day went up to Reno to meet Giannini on his return from New York. McFadden's wife recounted that, riding back with Giannini on the train, he got a great story. After he left the *Journal*, she said, he was "handling things that people went into bankruptcy over, packers, and so forth." The *Packing* newsletter followed. *Trucking* came a little later.

Eleanor grew up in Tacoma and worked in Seattle for a radio station. She and Din, as she called her husband, met on a blind date and dance at the Olympic Hotel. He was tall, dark and handsome and stole a kiss that first night.

I found McFadden delightful for his freshness of expression. When he was having trouble with his typewriter he was contrite: "It's my fault. I pound it so hard it bleats in alarm."

Recognizing the reworking and polishing that goes into any finished piece, he wrote one day: "That issue was so smooth I knew there was blood on the typewriter keys." There could have been no greater compliment. "Blood on the typewriter keys" lingers as a telling phrase.

A holiday, he sputtered at the addition of another national day off, "is just another damn day with no mail and no checks."

McFadden conceded that he murdered the king's English, but he talked the language of his subscribers, especially in *Trucking*. He recognized that the men emerging at the top in the consolidations in this industry had themselves begun behind the steering wheel. My father-in-law, Frank Lyman, a self-made retired grocer and meat-market operator who knew nothing about trucking, delighted in coming to my office and chuckling over the latest issue of *Trucking*.

Some of McFadden's choice bits came as a way to open a topic and give it breadth. In *Trucking*, finance was "the nice term for the art of having folding money when you need it." Mergers, he said, were "often referred to as the technique of believing you can make better money in any other deal than your own."

In talking about the uncertainty of mergers: "Guys who feel that they are just a couple of inches away from a nice, round finders fee, in both instances are talking optimistically but there is a quaver in their voices, too."

On the touchy competition of new imports of canned and dried fruit: "While nobody will talk about this and for a canner to be caught reading a letter from some other country is pretty much like spitting on the flag, it is being done."

Another time: "Management, that indefinable quality that comes in all sizes, shapes and colors continues to make the difference in western trucking." That same issue laid out a growing problem of pilferage from trucks: "In the old days the way to keep freight in the box was to back it up against a building or a wall. Also an old timer often could do the same job against a phone pole but it was a little more difficult. Whether it is side doors or drivers who dont take the trouble, the opening job seems to be about as tough as finding your way into an all night coffee stop. One shipper in the days when beer trucks used to take the boat up to Vallejo says he used to figure that he could count on being 3 bottles short and 6 if the guy found a friend on board. Now he says, the disappearing act is changed to the case basis and not one case, either."

After my daughter Marcia, who had spent a college year at the London School of Economics and was starting as a Kelly girl in San

Francisco, had Thanksgiving dinner at the McFaddens, he wrote: "I put her thru a little quizzing and find that the field of International Relations is sort of a glorified deal that I think sometime I took as commercial geography."

When I told McFadden that I was not getting a copy of *Trucking*, he replied: "Have checked and you are still a member of the club in good standing, cant understand why the hell you dont get copies, but there are a great many things in this world that baffle me and the Post Office is only one."

McFadden's *Packing* carried every whisker of detail he could get on the quantity of frozen or canned foods, product by product, put up in the West. When the National Association of Frozen Food Packers in Washington, D.C., came out with greatly improved detail for the Pacific Northwest, McFadden spotted this as the work of Tom House, who had moved up from the California to the national association. House, he reported, "not only is a guy with considerable personal charm, but he never turns it on unless he is pitching a deal that makes complete sense on its own hook. This might seem to be a small matter but it also is a knack a lot of top brass never seem to have mastered."

McFadden set himself to an office rule of "handle it only once." It was a discipline he applied to the mail and whatever else came onto his desk. The rule said in effect: "Make your decision now and get on to the next job. Don't clutter your desk or your mind. Don't stumble over yourself."

It's a good rule, I found, and a hard taskmaster. Universal, it can apply to almost anything you do. In the kitchen, for example, don't leave on the counter the empty pot you just finished with or the container of flour you just dipped from. Keep working surfaces clear. Women who cook a lot may scoff, but the rule holds. Cooking is essentially a matter of moving and processing materials, the same as in a machine shop.

I talked face to face to McFadden only three times in my life — once in that initial meeting in San Francisco and twice long afterward when he and Eleanor passed through Seattle on vacation and I took them for sightseeing and chatter.

Our acquaintanceship was by mail. For this very reason I think we were closer and understood each other better than if our link had been the telephone. It is so easy to pick up the phone, speak casually, and leave no record. But in letter writing a person has to think out what to say and then say it precisely. Writing also leaves a record to come back to.

As an example, when I was rassling with the idea of launching with Karl Hobson a farm price letter, I wanted McFadden's perspective. I set out in a "Dear Mac" letter the concept, the market, the partnership arrangement, and the burden that I'd be taking on. My letter ran to nearly three pages. It forced me to be precise, and it gave McFadden something to mull over before responding. He was the only person I turned to for guidance on what would be the biggest venture since starting the business newsletter.

Correspondence with McFadden built mutual respect, warm and deep, that carried for a quarter century to his death in the mid-70s. No person had greater influence in the years I published the newsletter. Indeed, when I was struggling to get the first 100 subscribers he kept me going with a flood of ideas, suggestions and encouragement from one who had traveled the same unposted valley.

In turn, as a free-lance reporter I kept a flow of news going to him for his two letters. He relished any tidbits I could send to answer the question How's Business, a question that began each issue of *Trucking* and was implicit in page 1 of *Packing*. He also welcomed anything for "Names are News" that ran at the bottom of each page. From me he counted mostly on the profile of a company — who, what and why. This forced me to get out and talk to people, and especially for *Packing* to learn about the food industry, so basic in my own work.

Even *Trucking* turned up bits that I could use. Once I stopped to get the profile of a Tacoma company that had five tank trucks hauling petroleum products, mainly to Fort Lewis. At a time of rising costs, the company surprisingly had petitioned to lower the rate to Fort Lewis. Why? I found the owner-operator on his back under a truck, greasy and fussing. Why the cut? Simple; he didn't want a pipeline to take that business away.

McFadden often ended suggestions for my newsletter with a topic to run down for his two sheets. Sometimes there was also a laugh. Telling of a complaint from the sales manager of New England Fish Co., McFadden could not help growling, "Not a sub, the bastards."

Farther down the page came a typical request: "You might give me a rundown on LA-Seattle [Motor Express] for Jan. 10 issue. It has been quite a while since we had them and if the gross and net is both up would make good stuff. If they are hauling more freight but fewer schedules on account [of] bigger boxes, that should be included. Also any way that they have worked out to improve the balance in the movement which I suppose is heavily northbound would be good to include."

Each June he wanted a quick telephone check on the likely size of the pack of frozen peas in the two-state Blue Mountain district centered at Walla Walla. This was the largest source of frozen peas in the nation, and the size and quality of the pack set the market. Weather was always a concern. If a spell of torrid 100-degree sunshine hit before the Fourth of July the harvest of green peas would end, brand-name buyers would have to scurry elsewhere, and growers would have to recover as best they could from a later harvest of dry peas. Whatever I found made news for both of us.

The newsletter was still groping along when McFadden took apart my latest sales letter and wrote out an alternative to be signed by the fictitious Jack Dalton, business manager. "My news services are going to hell and I am sitting down writing a sample letter for you," he began. "I have coined the name Jack Dalton, curse him, to be your business manager. Another guy can always say things about the *Roundup* that you would be embarrassed (or should be) to say.

"I dont like your letter, 'Are You Posted?' It looks so damn nice, it seems that maybe you printed up a million of them. A mimeographed letter would be sloppy but wouldnt look so permanent. I have typed out a little letter that isnt as good as yours but has a different slant."

The slant emphasized the gathering of news and condensing into "a concise once-over on the top trends in the Pacific Northwest business world....That's what every reader gets when he picks up an issue of *Marple's Business Roundup*. No mystery, no back door entrance, no special tips, just hard work boiling down essential Northwest news, much of which never gets published anywhere else."

McFadden called it a "snob appeal that not too many people can either understand or properly evaluate, but you are looking for the 6% that can. Bastards that move their lips when they read go for that."

Then McFadden tossed in a bit as to where he came from: "When I was on the *Wall Street News* and later the *Journal* both of them gave 50% commission for selling subs. My salary never covered my needs so I had to sell a lot on the side. And when you sell a *Wall Street Journal* sub to a guy who has just lost his shirt on Cities Service [in the Depression] and are in effect just asking him to do it again, that's something. We even sold subs to busted guys on the basis that they would look better carrying a *Wall Street Journal* in their coat pocket with the name turned to the outside." He ended: "I am going to have to spend some time now telling myself how to run my business. Best of luck."

Jack Dalton thus knocked on my door. He never got in, but I gladly grabbed some of his ideas. They were valid and refreshing.

I talked at times with McFadden (via the typewriter) of my need for help even before I could afford to hire anyone. He knew so well the difficulty of getting a fit. Of himself at age 60 he said, "I may be making the first step to selling my sheets and maybe it will light the path for you." Then in the earliest mention of his health he added: "As I was stretched out on the floor of the office this noon for the half hour concession I make to rest a bum ticker I pondered your problem instead of my own." He went on to open a new angle of marketing for me, then signed off: "No charge for this. I'm just one of those bastards who tell other people how to run their business and I cant run my own."

His perception about people was sound. Just as a bit of conversation I wrote him that I had spent the better part of a day with a *Wall Street Journal* reporter from San Francisco who came to me looking for a job or a way to come back to his native Portland. McFadden sounded a caution: "Simply as a guess, I would say that your man in the 48-50 age bracket does not quite understand the employment situation for that age bracket....Also the aroma of being an ex-*Wall Street Journal* reporter wafts off rather quickly. I am speaking with experience on this."

I told McFadden that the longer the WSJ man talked, "the less impressed I am with him. He ain't venturesome. He's had a paycheck for so long he isn't willing to gamble on his own productivity." McFadden figured that the man would find jobs scarce enough that he'd come back to me. Instead he landed on the public payroll of a Portland anti-poverty program.

By now, McFadden was wearying of his own business. "Some days," he wrote, "if some person wants to pay me $1000 for the *Trucking* and take over the subscription liability, he would get knocked down in my rush to take him up. This is one of those days.

"Glad to hear your sub curve is on the up. Mine aint. Altho you feel you dont have a peg, you basically have a much wider field than I do. And both of my fields are on the shrinking side and I am in the position that if I can stay even I am running well."

In the search for a buyer, he added,"I have completely dropped any reference to the widening horizons of being your own boss. Somehow I cant seem to find it in my heart to say that and keep solemn."

McFadden was at his desk at 7 in the morning, and Eleanor said he was always home on time for dinner — in which respect he did better than I. At Lent he always gave up something in deference to his wife, a Catholic. One year it was cigars. McFadden's own derivation was Presbyterian; his father was president of a Presbyterian college in Ames, Iowa.

In business McFadden could be tough. He refused to pay advertising agencies the customary 15 percent commission when they sent insert sheets for *Packing* or *Trucking*. Instead, he sold advertising directly, such as to a manufacturer of food-processing machinery or a builder of truck-trailers. He said that ad agencies hated his guts, but he figured he did not need the agencies, and I suspect he resented what he saw as smugness.

When my wife Dot died McFadden wrote a very touching note, and he and Eleanor made a gift in Dot's name to their favorite Catholic charity, the Hanna School for Boys. He also sent me a thoughtful offer: In California, he said, "any death usually means locking up the deposit box, freezing brokerage accounts, bank accounts, etc." In case Washington law was similar he offered to send me a wire transfer of an interest-free loan for as long as I might want. Thanks ever so much but not necessary.

That "bum ticker" slowed McFadden. He sold *Trucking*, and before long it went out of business. Later he sold *Packing*. Hard to do, Eleanor said years later when Barbara (my second wife) and I visited her in a retirement home. "It was his baby and he had seen it grow," she said, "but he knew he had to sell." That publication expanded into the wine industry, and the masthead listed McFadden as assistant publisher. But he made no input and the reporting seemed hollow without his insight.

The McFaddens had no children. I don't recall ever hearing of family other than Eleanor's sister in Tacoma. As I look back at our long association, I think I may have served in some way as a son, someone whom McFadden might guide with the affection of a father and who might perhaps carry into another generation a bit of what McFadden had learned and stood for in his own life.

McFadden is dead, but he lives on in Marple's Business Newsletter. I reverence his memory.

Chapter Nine
Banks Make News

News often lies hidden. One day when Sam McFadden was in his prime and careless with the long-distance phone, he called me: "Do you know how to figure per-share bank earnings?" No, never heard of it. Then he sketched the technique, and I took notes as fast as he talked. McFadden, an underdog himself, relished pulling a good news story out from under people who thought they controlled their world.

In those days, small and regional banks liked to hold back the goodies about their earnings until the shareholders gathered at the annual meeting in February. But the bank regulator, the Comptroller of the Currency, required banks to publish promptly a bit of all-important detail — the year-end Statement of Condition. In the first week of January the *Daily Journal of Commerce* in Seattle and its counterpart in Portland ran a full page of these bank statements, handled as advertisements and as dull as anything in dullsville.

McFadden's call put meaning into the stark bank statements. Take the figure labeled "earned surplus," he said. Deduct the comparable figure from a year ago to get the year's gain (or loss). Add dividends and divide by the number of shares outstanding. This gives "indicated per share earnings," called "indicated" because they were not released by the bank. There were cautions, too: don't get tripped by stock splits and acquisitions.

I worked the detail out for the region's four big banks — Seattle-First National and Marine Bancorporation (holding company of National Bank of Commerce) in Seattle, and U.S. National and First National in Portland. I later added Pacific National, Seattle, which then distinguished itself by keeping out of the scramble for branches.

In time I included banks in Spokane, Boise and several secondary cities.

It was fun. To protect myself I walked over to the controller at each of the Seattle banks and asked, off the record, "How does my arithmetic look?" It was OK. I phoned to check out-of-town banks. I published the result. At first, just a short item on page 4, but it got attention. Perhaps the newsletter also drew a little more respect from a bank president when stockholders called to ask, what about these figures that Marple has?

In the second year of this series, the newsletter reported a surge in bank profits: "Our tabulation of indicated earnings per share, revealed in year-end statements, shows an average increase of 12%. For many NW banks 1953 earnings were the best in at least four years, and for some, new records." The region was growing; its banks were growing, and "more money was out on loans to business, to consumers, and in mortgages than ever before."

The newsletter's report expanded year by year to include more banks and to add detail. Here was a quick answer to a stockholder or a customer with the ever-present concern, how's my bank doing?

A four-year comparison of earnings told at a glance that five banks were on the upswing and two were not. The report also added two tell-tale indicators closely watched at that time — the ratio of deposits to loans and the ratio of deposits to capital funds. All the data came from the raw "Statement of Condition," but I talked to a lot of bankers for the analysis of what lay back of the raw figures and what might lie ahead.

"What happens to bank earnings," the newsletter reported, "has importance well beyond financial institutions. For Pacific NW banks, good earnings have been essential to promote growth in capital and expansion in loans to business. Pacific NW banks have consistently plowed back a large part of their earnings to provide additional capital."

The growth in earnings and stability of the region's economy also made bank stocks increasingly attractive to investors. As a result the newsletter added to the tabulation a column to show market price and said: "Stocks of some of the larger Pacific NW banks ended the year with gains of from 30% to almost 50%....Ownership of stocks in major Pacific NW banks has been widening in recent years. Buying has come from investors in California and the East."

Banks found themselves squeezed to keep up with growth in the economy: "Banks may have to reduce their holdings of government bonds in order to obtain additional funds for loans. [Conservative] banks which like to keep their ratio of loans to deposits around 48%, for example, may find that ratio reaching 55%. This shift of funds from low-interest government bonds to higher-interest commercial loans of course will improve earnings."

During the Depression banks paid as little as 1.5% on savings. Rates continued at bottom during World War II, and consumers put free cash instead into patriotic and higher-paying government savings bonds. Then as the economy surged in the 1950s savings began to pay better.

Essentially, savings deposits provided banks and savings & loan associations money to lend on residential construction and mortgages. Housing continued short as people moved into the Pacific Northwest. Builders needed financing. Pacific First Federal Savings & Loan Association, Tacoma, biggest S&L in the NW and 10th in the U.S., jumped its interest rate in July 1950 to 2.5%. In one year its savings grew 28%, the greatest, the newsletter reported, of any NW savings institution. Pacific First had offices in five cities of Washington and Oregon. Much of its growth came in Portland. There Oregon's two statewide banks pushed their rates up, too, but slowly. U.S. National offered 2.5% on a three-year savings certificate. First National bounced back with full-page newspaper advertisements. "In less hallowed halls," the newsletter reported, "the competition would be tagged a rate war." By contrast, savings deposits in Seattle banks, clinging to 1.5%, shrank.

As banks and savings & loans stepped up the fight for savings, the newsletter inaugurated an annual and later semi-annual tabulation and analysis of savings by state and by type of institution. It was a grueling task to gather the *what* from state and federal regulatory agencies and to check with leaders in the industry for the *why*.

Our first summary, in mid-1952, placed total savings deposits in the four-state region at nearly $2 billion, up more than $200 million in a year. The biggest gains came not at commercial banks but at mutual savings banks and the tough kid on the block, savings & loan associations, aggressive in promotion of savings and in lending to builders.

The flow of money into savings accounts had wide implications, the newsletter reported, "plain enough indication that retailers are competing not only among each other for consumer dollars but also with well-promoted savings institutions." By 1959 the four-state total in savings reached almost $3.9 billion, up $417 million in a year. S&Ls alone accounted for almost half the growth.

Somewhat parallel to the series on savings deposits was the newsletter series on building permits, a monthly tabulation gathered from a dozen cities and counties. The report covered office buildings, warehouses and manufacturing plants. It also broke out residential construction that tied so closely to savings accounts.

Wanting to be as current as possible I gathered the figures directly from the building departments that issued the permits. For this I used a reply post card or a telephone call when on a deadline. The information covered Portland, Spokane and Seattle, their counties (unincorporated areas surrounding these cities), plus Tacoma, Yakima, Walla Walla, Missoula, Boise, Eugene and Salem. Out of this came a glimpse of a significant part of the economy in diverse sections of the Pacific Northwest.

Looking back I am surprised how quickly the material was pulled together. Several times when the first of the month fell on Monday, I gathered the data by phone on that day for the month just closed, and subscribers had the information in their hands when the newsletter reached them on Wednesday. Building permits foreshadowed construction months ahead and were a guide also to suppliers of construction materials and home furnishings.

The first tabulation revealed residential construction in March 1951 down 37% from a year earlier and total construction down by almost a half. Why? "The NW building industry is beginning to show the effects of government restrictions" in the Korean war — credit controls in residential construction and conservation of critical building materials in commercial construction.

Nearly two years passed before government constraints fell away. By 1958-59 building permits foreshadowed a surge in the region's economy carrying into the next decade. The newsletter ran the tabulation whenever the year-ago comparison was significant. The trend thus revealed often became part of the newsletter's page-one look-ahead.

In time the series was dropped, in a sense a casualty of the very growth the early years had chronicled. Construction, notably residential, was moving to the suburbs. Annexation was changing city boundaries. New cities were being carved out of areas whose building permits formerly were masked in county totals. The quick data and year-ago comparison lost meaning. The newsletter turned to other sources for the trend — checking directly with builders and their trade associations, keeping tabs on the flow of mortgage money, and looking for early signs on large construction projects.

The series on bank earnings and the quite separate series on savings deposits grew and blossomed for some 40 years, then ran afoul of the sweep toward nationwide banking. Cross-state mergers and acquisitions in the 1980s and 1990s made continuity of reporting impossible. The downtown corner bank, once a landmark in every city and town, lost identity and sometimes even its presence. The two largest banks in Washington state became outposts of California banks. The large statewide banks in Oregon and Idaho merged into out-of-state financial institutions.

So sweeping were mergers and acquisitions that the Federal Reserve Bank of San Francisco gave up its weekly report of assets and liabilities of "large commercial banks and domestic subsidiaries." That publication had been a fixture in bank management for decades. But by mid-1997 the San Francisco Federal Reserve recognized that its summary for the West was rendered meaningless by "the ability of banks to establish branches virtually nationwide."

Similar convulsion hit savings banks and their one-time rivals, the savings & loan associations. The half century after World War II was the era of S&Ls. They promoted savings as commercial banks did not, paid a higher rate of interest to attract deposits, and lent primarily on residential mortgages. When the stock market panted for new issues, many S&Ls issued stock and became publicly held institutions with broader lending power. Mergers and consolidations followed.

The very definition of savings changed. Consumer dollars that once went into savings banks or S&Ls often flow now into tax-advantaged individual retirement accounts and from there into mutual funds or directly into the stock market. Stock brokers in turn offer customers what amount to interest-paying savings accounts for funds awaiting investment. How big these newer savings are, state by state, no one knows; there are no published data.

And who would have thought that Washington Mutual, for three-quarters of a century a conventional savings bank having no stockholders, would convert to a corporation with stock held by thousands of investors across the country, a financial powerhouse with branches as distant as California and Florida?

Chapter Ten
The Service Industries

Growth in manufacturing in the broadening economy brought a parallel growth in services. "One industry of expanding importance in the Pacific NW," the newsletter reported as early as 1953, "is insurance — companies with home offices in this region that write fire, casualty, or life policies. The industry has grown far larger than is commonly recognized and...is one of the most stable of all business, in good times and bad."

By 1953 the Pacific Northwest had 26 insurance companies, each with assets of at least $1 million. As reported at the time, "a key factor in their growth is the virility of young, aggressive companies that began as underdog...and pioneered new types of policies."

The smokeless factories of insurance companies provide a steady payroll. Beyond this they retain or bring into the region millions of dollars invested notably in tax-free municipal bonds of school, water, local improvement districts, and other units of government.

Expansion came in the 1960s with organization of new companies to write life insurance. Many began by serving just their immediate area, then pushed into other states, unhampered by freight costs so critical to manufacturing. By 1970 the region had 33 life insurance companies, their annual income $223 million, their assets $758 million. New life companies, the newsletter reported, "eat up lots of capital during their early years. Sales, medical and other expenses of putting a policy on the books, plus reserves, exceed total premiums from the first years of the policy. A company does well if it makes money in its first seven years."

Mergers and acquisitions followed in insurance as in banking. There are fewer companies but of greater assets. Much the largest in the Pacific Northwest is the Safeco group in Seattle. It began in 1923 as General Insurance Co., writing fire and casualty insurance. It added life insurance in 1957 and mutual funds in the 1980s. The company now ranks itself "among the largest diversified financial corporations in America." In 1999 it employs 12,000 nationwide. Its revenues approach $7 billion a year, its assets total $31 billion.

Computers came early to the Pacific Northwest, long before Microsoft and Micron Technology; indeed, before Bill Gates was born. *Applications* came first; some of the region's leading banks, insurance companies and utilities bought computers made elsewhere in the country as they sought ways to hold down operating costs. Soon *manufacture* took hold — tools such as oscilloscopes, critical parts such as transistors, and hardware such as control systems in aircraft. Finally came the design and production of *software* by Microsoft and dozens of Pacific Northwest companies building brains for computers.

The newsletter's first recognition of computers came more than 40 years ago. Under the headline "Mechanical Brains Move In" a two-page report in 1956 cited half a dozen installations. One of these, Pacific Power & Light (now PacifiCorp), Portland, shifted from manual billing of 300,000 customers to "electronic computing and printing of bills. Savings in labor alone offset the substantial capital outlay."

General Insurance Co. (now Safeco) put in electronic data processing that was becoming common in large life insurance companies. General, the newsletter said, was "the first fire and casualty company in America with this equipment." I recall how officials of General proudly showed off their computer. It took up the space of a ballroom, and before the days of the computer chip its innumerable vacuum tubes required an elaborate cooling system. Remarkable as that computer was, it could not match the work of a simple personal computer of the 1990s.

"The first jobs assigned to electronic computers," the newsletter explained, "generally have to do with company overhead — payrolls and accounting. Here the economics are demonstrable and appeal to those who hold the company's purse strings. But those who work with computers contend that the big field is in management-science where management uses a computer, for example, for closer scheduling and coordination of production."

A year later the newsletter found manufacture in electronics "leveling off for the first time in a half-dozen years" but still "probably the fastest growing industry in the Pacific NW." Portland was the center; the largest of a half-dozen in manufacture was Tektronix, builder of oscilloscopes in a $1-million plant at Beaverton. On Seattle's north side was John Fluke Manufacturing and on the east side United Control Corp., founded by four Boeing engineers to make systems for aircraft, "selling nationwide and overseas." Shares of Tektronix, Fluke and United Control were publicly traded.

Getting skilled help was a problem, then and now. In early days there was "no pool of trained help...but turnover at Portland and Seattle is exceptionally low, and morale is high....In recruiting engineers and scientists the attraction of the Pacific NW as a place to live proves helpful." The need was for "engineers and mathematicians, and particularly those with the curious combination of an ability to think logically and the personality of a salesman."

Readers looked for more reporting on this gangling new industry. An encouraging note from W.P. Dyke, Linfield Research Institute, McMinnville, said a recent issue "covers in excellent fashion the Northwest's expansion in electronics...lucid and comprehensive."

Computer applications spread. In 1958 banks were beginning to imprint magnetic code on checks. U.S. National Bank in Portland was out front, "the first bank in the nation to put into operation automatic check-handling equipment." It was mailing coded checks to customers at the rate of 17,000 a month. The arithmetic was unbeatable: "Bankers figure that automatic check-handling is as inevitable as the dial was to the telephone business. Automation will shift drudgery to machines and in the long run should cut costs in the face of the continual increase in flow of checks."

That was 40 years ago. Since then the emergence of dozens of new companies, each with a specialty, established the Pacific Northwest as a designer and builder of software with markets worldwide. All this in an industry so young, so ambitious, so resourceful.

Chapter Eleven
Hobson's Farm Forecast

One of the earliest fans of the newsletter was Karl Hobson, a farm economist at the Agricultural Extension Service in Pullman, Washington. The Extension Service, a federal agency created to help farmers, is attached to Washington State University, where Hobson also did some teaching.

I don't remember how we first met. Most likely I took his name from a news release and dropped him a note asking for more background or reasons-why. One day when he was in Seattle he looked me up. He was perhaps a year or two older than I; a bit taller, with black hair and trim, athletic build. He had a gentle but earnest way of speaking; I never heard him swear. He had a searching mind. I soon saw that he brought to his study of price and supply of farm products an unshaken independence. When the facts he had gathered warranted, he delighted in quietly bucking the accepted wisdom.

Hobson chafed under the constraints that a government institution placed on forecasts that might unsettle sensitive markets. He thought there must be a place for a private newsletter that would go beyond government estimates of acreage or tonnage and guide a grower as to the prices to expect at harvest.

The Pacific Northwest had no such publication. The nearest was Doane Agricultural Services in St. Louis. It focused heavily on the Midwest and South but was light on specialized products of the Pacific Northwest. At various times Karl and I, some 300 miles apart at opposite ends of the state, swapped ideas about launching a newsletter. Karl was itching to write a private farm-price forecast but had no way to publish or sell it. Would I join him by taking on the printing, distribution, and sale of subscriptions?

The idea was intriguing, as much an innovation as my business newsletter, then in its second year. My part of a farm newsletter, I figured, should not take too much time or interfere with my newsletter's exacting publishing schedule. Karl was restless. Early in 1951 he said he was ready, and I said yes. Thus began *Hobson's Farm Forecast*, an equal partnership and a by-product or supplement to the work each of us was already doing. Neither of us expected to get rich, but it would be fun, and who knew where it might lead?

The *Forecast*, usually four pages, focused on help for a farmer at decision-time. Our initial offering by mail carried the line: "Will you get top prices?" It promised to cover the wide range of Pacific Northwest crops and livestock. The most important were potatoes, of which Idaho was the nation's largest producer. But the letter would include also highly specialized crops such as dry peas and dry beans, of which Idaho and Washington produce most of the nation's supply. There would be reports also on wheat, onions, hay, alfalfa seed, clover seed, beef cattle, hogs, sheep, eggs, and even the price of farm land itself. For a few products such as apples, peaches or cherries there would be less to say; the orchardist had made his decision when he set out his trees.

Karl saw an unusual opportunity in potatoes as 1951 opened. Two years of overproduction had brought disastrous prices. Government price supports were coming off potatoes. Growers, discouraged by losses, would cut back new plantings, go light on fertilizer, and put their better soil into other crops. Bankers, badly burned the previous year, would hold down on financing. All told, Karl said, the crop was

HOBSON'S FARM FORECAST
A Private Analysis Prepared by Karl Hobson for Northwest Farmers

Published by MARPLE'S BUSINESS ROUNDUP
407 Bay Building, Seattle 1, Washington

sure to be small and prices high. Indeed, the government report on intended plantings suggested the smallest acreage since 1873. This was the time to plunge with a forecast.

Neither Karl nor I had the money to quit our jobs and go full time on the farm letter. But we felt that with the expenditure of time and very little money we could test the potential. So we started as part-timers. The Extension Service helped with a concession: Hobson could remain full-time on its staff and moonlight on his private forecast as long as he did not sell to subscribers in Washington state. That was fine with us. Idaho was a big market that Karl knew well. He had graduated from the University of Idaho, followed up with a master's degree in agricultural economics, and worked several years for the Idaho Extension Service. Idaho thus became our testing ground. We started there and in potato areas of Oregon and Colorado.

We called the letter *Hobson's Farm Forecast*. The masthead carried the line: "A Private Analysis Prepared by Karl Hobson for Northwest Farmers." Then, for identification: "Published by Marple's Business Roundup." We recognized that we should have our address in the farm country instead of a distant industrial city, but that was a compromise we had to put up with.

The subscription was $12 a year. Doane's letter, as I recall, was $15 a year. The *Forecast*, usually four pages, came out at least once in two weeks, more often when news warranted. We turned out 28 issues the first year, 41 the next. These included a number of special reports devoted to a single crop or livestock.

Karl wrote in longhand and mailed his forecast to me. He never learned to type, and this was years before personal computers ruled the world. I took his forecast to Ethel Shelton's letter shop to type and print, and I brought the copies back to the newsletter office to mail. There, with temporary help sometimes standing and sometimes sitting on stools at the big drafting tables, we stuffed envelopes and hurried the mailing off to the post office.

We began our search for customers with a deliberately low-pressure sales letter that described the *Forecast* and enclosed an introductory offer. We mailed at bulk rates to all RFD (rural free delivery) mail boxes in towns that Hobson, from long knowledge of Idaho farming, had carefully selected. A fair bit of this mail we knew would go into the wastebaskets of non-farmers, but with postage at one cent apiece we could afford a little waste. In the late 1990s, postage alone would have run close to 20 cents apiece, prohibitive for this type of marketing.

The response? Well, we didn't know what to expect. But there were indeed some subscribers, 489 by the end of that first year, and we were sure that Hobson's forecast of big money in potatoes — which proved right on the nose — would bring in more. All through the year, issue after issue, Hobson turned out forecasts of markets for one product after another, forecasts that we could trumpet in sales mail. Typically:

Beef Cattle: A year ago Hobson warned that a drop in beef cattle prices was coming. In midwinter he forecast the spring break in the price of fed cattle — in time so that our subscribers could sell before the drop. The actual amount of the break was correctly predicted in the February 21 Forecast at $2 to $4.

Eggs: Last winter the Hobson's Forecast pointed out that a profitable year was ahead for egg production. This was in plenty of time to get chicks early.

Hogs: In December the Forecast said that the next few months would see little advance in hog prices. On March 14, the Forecast said: "Some time in May hog prices will start advancing again. They will go up pretty steadily until late August or early September. There is a good chance that they will go to about $25." If you have followed the hog market, you know that that is almost exactly what happened.

Karl regarded his forecasts as predictions, not recommendations. He wanted to supply information as a guide to decision making. He built his estimates from an extraordinary range of data, an understanding of the producer and his markets, and a wide acquaintanceship among farmers and ranchers. His objective was to help on decisions. Should a grower, for example, contract to sell the crop when he was putting seed in the ground, or gamble on the cash market at harvest? And if he gambled with a crop such as wheat, potatoes or dry peas that could go into storage, how long after harvest should he hold?

"We will not raise your batting average to 100 percent," Karl wrote subscribers in that first year. "That is impossible in this business where some factors are unpredictable. But we can boost it from 40 or 50 percent to about 80 percent — and that means money in the bank for you."

The presentation of the farm letter picked up lessons from the business letter. When Karl had so much to include that he wanted to go beyond four pages, I countered: "I feel strongly that four single-spaced typewritten pages is as much as a man will sit still for at one reading....

"Also, as one who wears the hairshirt of the *Roundup* [as the business letter was then still called], I am certain that the discipline of brevity compressed to four pages is good, and that having to cut and fit into that space makes what goes into it a lot more important and more effective." I cited a report I had just finished on the expansion of British Columbia industry and said that whatever that "report is worth is the result not from the fact that I had enough material to fill a half-dozen issues solid, but that I had to leave 80% of this out. That was the most difficult piece of work I've done since I started the *Roundup*, and I was so sick of the stuff when I got through that I haven't yet been able to look at it. But had I written it long I'd have lost readers."

In talking about renewals, my letter to Karl continued, "I think the material you have turned out is good. The only reservation I have had all along is whether we are making the *Forecast* appear exclusive enough....The *Forecast* should be the sort that a fellow almost checks to see that no one else in the room is looking when he starts to read it.

"Your judicious use of the first person in writing is good, one way of helping get the impressive direct connection that we want....

"Wherever we can we ought to draw conclusions wider than the product being talked about. If there is something in the wool picture that is of meaning to a spud grower, we ought always point up these wider implications. E.g., I am going to run some guff in the next *Roundup* on appliance sales. I haven't figured out how to handle this yet, but I've got to get something in there so that the man selling chemicals or lumber won't say, 'To hell with this; I don't sell appliances.' I'm going to make the troubles that appliances have run into a warning to producers of all consumer goods — if I can."

Karl's longhand copy often needed editing to fit the space or to bring out emphasis. He gave me a free hand. "I am amazed," he wrote, "at how much you can work my copy over and not do violence to the meaning." Another time: "I certainly appreciate help on the land special, although I am sorry that you had to spend so much time on it. You apologize for not understanding the subject matter more. Actually, I am lucky that you don't. If you were an economist you would be no help on things like this."

Hobson's Farm Forecast, still just a sideline, perked right along. At the close of the second year we had 1,257 subscribers — not as wild as tumbleweed rolling across the desert, but we kept expenses down and began taking out profit on a 50-50 basis.

We had confidence now to expand. Karl resigned from the Extension Service and, working at home, went full-time on the *Forecast*.

This lifted the blackout on our selling in Washington state, and new subscriptions there should enable Karl to draw compensation equal to at least what he had been getting at the Extension Service. The Forecast also could now carry Karl's address and phone number. In the division of salary and earnings, two parts went to Hobson, one to Marple.

We incorporated as Hobson's Farm Forecast, Inc. That gave us the flexibility of a corporation in place of a cumbersome partnership. It also provided protection in the unlikely circumstance of a subscriber's suing over a disappointing forecast — something that never happened.

In setting up the corporation I had the assistance of George Orton, who had moved from California with his family and, like a number of others, popped into the newsletter office one day looking for leads to business opportunities. Orton kindly set up the accounts for the new corporation, a task for which I had no training.

Karl and I had complete confidence in each other, and there was never a financial issue between us. But I wanted the financial records so clear that someone could step into the business end of the *Forecast* without a flicker of question. Orton's accounts called for a numbered voucher for each check I wrote — and I wrote all the checks.

We stepped up our marketing and in a year doubled the number of subscribers. We continued pushing sales mail to rural boxholders before planting time, and in our second year sent out 60,000 pieces of mail. The three individuals working part-time stuffing envelopes with this sales mail averaged close to 70 years in age, a dependable, grateful crew, chattering as they worked together.

Karl also developed a new approach to selling. He hired a couple of college students to go to county courthouses and pick from assessors' rolls the names and addresses of large landholders, many of whom lived in a town and therefore would not get our mail to rural boxholders. In some counties we also picked up names of those with a large inventory of farm machinery; they were renters and good prospects.

The courthouse records gave us a way to reach potato growers in the rich Red River Valley of North Dakota and Minnesota. Karl visited some of these areas and talked with growers, and we tailored our sales mail to the crops in a given area. In California we concentrated on growers of early potatoes and onions. We mailed in one year, 1954, to 20,500 names from courthouse records. In that year we had 2,400 subscribers in a dozen states.

Karl also drew encouraging personal attention. Elon J. Gilbert, president of Richey & Gilbert, Yakima, a leader in the fruit industry, wrote: "I have admired the courage with which your forecasts are made and wonder if there is any chance you would like to consider a position in the fruit industry." No, thanks! A little later Gilbert said in effect: "You should develop the consulting business. The *Forecast* will be your bread and butter; consulting will provide the cream." That, incidentally, was the pattern of Doane Agricultural Services, our big competitor; farm management, not its newsletter, was the heart of its business. Karl also was offered an attractive government spot in agricultural economics in Washington, D.C. The answer was the same: No, thanks!

Our experiment, so gingerly launched three years earlier, came to a turning point in 1954. The *Forecast* had grown in reputation, in number of customers and in prospects. But that growth also made more apparent to Karl and me that we'd have to do a major reorganization that neither of us wanted. It simply was no longer feasible to operate with the two functions — editorial and marketing — 300 miles apart. Karl, working alone, needed to talk over the forecasts he was developing, the response of customers, and areas where the *Forecast* should grow. I, working alone, needed Karl's help on marketing, the handling of renewals, and the layout of sales materials. Clearly, we also needed a full-time business manager.

Karl's location in Pullman became an endless frustration in communications. Karl and I had an almost daily flow of letters back and forth, and I hung on the postman when I knew the draft of the next *Forecast* should be on its way. But there was no direct mail between Pullman and Seattle; Pullman mail went through Spokane. We tried airmail, we tried special delivery, and Karl often drove to the Pullman railroad station with a letter to go with the train to Spokane for transfer to a train going to Seattle.

Karl had to send his lists of prospects to me for mailing. I had to send back to him the names of subscribers and renewals as they came in so that he could monitor and tailor our next sales push. It was awkward. We needed to work side by side, but we saw no way to get together. Karl had to be in an agricultural center such as Pullman. I had to remain in Seattle or abandon my business news service — the newsletter and reporting for national publications. We also needed to add professional and clerical staff.

There were other considerations. Karl saw a tighter year ahead for the farm economy, and that would be tough on renewals. Forecasting also takes a toll on the forecaster. From the outset Karl had said that he could not hit 100 percent. But a forecast that missed the mark hurt.

Yes, there were warm notes such as from a grower in Riverton, Wyoming: "Your forecasts on potatoes has made me lots of money. I cannot be without your advice." But almost in the same mail to me was Karl's candid comment: "What bothers me most about the *Forecast* are busts like the current one on dry peas. There's no way of preventing them. The one on alsike clover two years ago was similar. I suppose I should hedge more, but of course that would be watering the stuff down. In the Extension Service I just avoided going out on shaky limbs. By being definite and specific only on the ones that were pretty safe I gained a reputation for being bold and specific but accurate." Glumly, he added also: "I hesitate to think about going through life tied to this 7-day week on the *Forecast*."

By now we had spread as far as Nebraska, almost into the front yard of Doane Agricultural Services, our only competitor. Doane clearly was uneasy. When we pushed into California, Doane opened an office in Sacramento. Before long it came to us with an offer to buy the *Forecast*. About the same time the Extension Service at Pullman wanted Karl back — at increased responsibility and salary.

We talked at length with Doane and then sold. *Hobson's Farm Forecast* ceased publication in July 1955. Doane brought out a new publication, "Doane's Western Farm Forecast, formerly Hobson's Farm Forecast." To discharge our responsibility to our customers Karl wrote for one year for Doane's new publication. Two years later Doane abandoned its western farm forecast.

We were happy. Karl figured that his salary and share of earnings from the *Forecast* came to nearly twice the salary he had been getting at the Extension Service. He had learned a lot, too, he wrote me; "had a great deal of fun, and one of the most enjoyable parts was working with you."

For my part the *Forecast* had boosted my income at the critical beginning of the business letter. By now the business letter was growing fast enough so that within a year its new subscribers more than offset the earnings I had been getting from the *Forecast*.

How successful were we? At our peak we had 2,400 subscribers. That sounds small, but a conservative estimate of gross income of the farms we served suggests that we were guiding the sale of well over $200 million a year in farm products. The amount may well have been greater; our customers were mostly the larger producers.

I know of no private farm forecast launched in the Pacific Northwest since *Hobson's*. In retrospect, Elon Gilbert was right in his Dutch uncle advice to Karl: the *Farm Forecast* should go beyond its focus on markets and move into farm management — working out with an owner or tenant the products to raise, the adaptability of the soil, fertilizing, financing, marketing and dozens of decisions all through the year. But that would have called for money and staff that we did not have and was far beyond our personal interest.

Karl retired from the Extension Service in 1971. He received a number of awards, such as a bronze plaque from the Federal Land Bank of Spokane for "outstanding contributions to American agriculture." For many years Karl suffered from various food allergies that greatly restricted his diet and would have sidelined a less determined person. Late in retirement he found relief in what he ascribed to the exercise of sheer will power.

When Karl and his wife retired to Maui for his health he wrote: "Here's hoping we can keep in touch. I can truthfully say, Elliot, that I have enjoyed my association with you more than any other I have had." It was mutual.

Karl died in 1986, age 80.

CHAPTER TWELVE
Help Wanted

The newsletter was for much too long a one-man shop. Yes, help was wanted — to some extent as extra eyes and ears for news, but to a greater extent in running the office. The burden grew as the list of subscribers grew.

For help on news I kept in touch with four or five stringers. One was Ray Bloomberg, the full-time Seattle correspondent for McGraw-Hill publications other than *Business Week*. He focused heavily on construction tradepapers. We swapped ideas or observations from time to time, and I think I gave him more help than he gave me. He would never take any pay. He did, however, look out for *Business Week* one summer month when I was away.

Louis Huber, Seattle, a free-lance producer of educational films on Alaska, kept me alert to what was happening in that state. He also wrote occasionally for the daily *Christian Science Monitor* — a feather in any reporter's cap. On his pushing I wrote occasionally about the Pacific Northwest for the *Monitor*. Huber was an unyielding grammarian who combed through every issue of the newsletter.

Much the most helpful of my stringers — and, sorry to say, I did not pay them much — was Florence Millsaps in Portland (later Mrs. Bill Jenkins). She grew up in a small town in Idaho and came out of the Depression strong and resourceful. When her job in the business office of the *Butte Standard* died in the Depression, she left for Portland, got a job at the *Oregon Journal* selling classified ads and went to night law school. In time she became secretary to the publisher, the highest paid woman on the paper. When women reporters got a boost through the Newspaper Guild to a higher salary than Florence's, she chose instead of grousing at the publisher to beat the pack with extra work as a stringer for tradepapers. One of her papers was *Advertising Age*. I looked her up one day when I was in Portland. She sent me news items from Portland and subsequently when she and her husband lived in Klamath Falls and later ran a weekly paper in eastern Oregon. She was good at spotting unusual incidents that illustrated something bigger taking place. Another stringer in Portland was Jim Conroy, the homespun founder and publisher of *Chain Saw Age*.

There was no question I needed a full-time reporter, but I saw no way to pay for one. I became so strapped for time that one month I cut tradepapers almost to zero and skimped on *Business Week*. I wrote Dick McCarty in San Francisco, "I can easily spend full time on the farm letter....What licks me is seeing any economical way to hire help for *BW* and tradepapers. In this biz a man can work himself long hours that he would never ask another person to work and come up with about [the Newspaper] Guild pay scale. There just isn't margin to hire a man [or woman] — whether he is paid a weekly salary and I keep the money for space rates, or is paid the magazine's space rates less X% for my overhead and direction. I am groping for an answer where I am inclined to think there is none."

Office work clung to me for the first couple of years. I kept the books, made out invoices, addressed envelopes, acknowledged every new subscription, and of course typed my own letters. I used to take home routine jobs like typing renewal notices, and after supper I'd work on a stack of 3x5 file cards for subscriptions expiring in the next month. I recall one year I was so far behind that it was already February and I had not yet sent out renewal notices for January, each one to a specific day. Should I try to collect a month late, or should I get current by giving January away? I decided to tough it out and, late as it was, bill for January. I found that being late didn't matter.

When the 905 Second Avenue Building, the old Burke Building, was to be torn down I moved in 1951 to the top floor of the Bay Building at First and University Street. It was a wood and brick structure, convenient on the edge of the downtown business core, but its better days were past.

It had opened in 1894 as the Arlington Hotel and later, we were told, housed the Seattle post office. Built on the edge of a steep hill, it was four stories from the First Avenue entrance up to the top floor, and four stories down to the alley on Post Street, almost at the level of the waterfront.

First Avenue was not a good business address — on the sleazy side with pawn shops, tattoo artists and Army and Navy surplus stores. I listed the address on the newsletter as the Bay Building. Most people did not know where that was and it sounded good.

Next to the entrance on First Avenue was a foul-smelling beer joint. A flight down brought you to the Garden of Allah, a notorious cabaret run by two gay men who put on shows with female impersonators and complained bitterly about police shakedowns. In Prohibition times the space housed a speakeasy.

On its upper floors the Bay Building had a number of large rooms for light manufacturing, but much of the space was empty. Near the elevator on our top floor was a shop making women's apparel. Down the hall was East's Bindery, run by Mr. East and Russ, his skilled assistant. The heart of this shop was a fascinating machine for ruling accounting paper with whatever arrangement of columns a business might specify. I recall it as almost as large as an automobile. The frame was of beautifully fashioned dark hardwood, suggestive of something out of the Victorian era. The machine, carefully tended, did very precise work, not by printing but by moving blank sheets of paper under an array of pens, each drawing its own line across the paper and each taking its ink from a tiny fountain of red, green, blue or whatever color the accountants called for.

More important for the newsletter was East's big folding machine, standard equipment in a bindery. Herm Jondal, my printer, delivered the newsletter in sheets 11 by 17 inches for East to fold. As soon as we heard the fast clackety-clack of the folding machine, we hustled down the hall to pick up a handful of newsletters and start stuffing envelopes that we had already addressed. We took the mail to the post office that afternoon.

The newsletter office had two adjoining rooms. The first room you came to from the elevator was the so-called "inside room" of hotel days. It had opaque windows that let in light from the hall. It had no outside windows but was convenient to a common washroom and toilet down the hall. A doorway opened to the "outside room," which also had a direct entrance around a zig of the hallway. The outside room had a tiny wash basin in one corner. The ceilings were high and the woodwork grimy with heavy paint from better times. Three tall windows looked out in silent grandeur to the Seattle harbor, Bainbridge Island and the distant snowy Olympic Mountains.

I delighted in that magnificent view, as fine as any in the city. My father-in-law, Frank Lyman, the retired Massachusetts grocer living with us, liked it too. He fished in Elliott Bay for salmon, then plentiful. On his way home from a boathouse in West Seattle he often stopped at the office to do some chores. Then he shopped for the family in the Pike Place Market, a couple of blocks north.

The Bay Building had no insulation. The top floor was hot in summer sun, but the windows opened wide. In winter after an unusually cold weekend the noisy steam radiators took all of Monday to yield enough heat for any one to peel off a sweater. The rent was cheap, $25 a month to start, then $35, unchanged for a decade.

The floor of the outside room was covered with heavy so-called battleship linoleum, probably surplus from World War I. One of my occasional Saturday chores required taking pail and water to the wooden floor of the inside room. The secretary who later joined me recalled the janitor who appeared now and then as "a nice man, not too helpful, who got mired in his own problems and couldn't get through his shift without a bottle for comfort."

By the time I moved into the Bay Building I could no longer put off hiring office help. On mailing day my wife, Dot, gladly came in, and also Frank Lyman. So did my aunt Catharine Jameson, then in her 80s. She came by bus, happy to have something useful to do. She was not fast but was dependable. What I paid her qualified her for Social Security and in time brought her the minimum Social Security check, $50 a month. Daughter Marcia, a college girl, worked one summer and learned to keep books.

By fall I needed a part-timer to handle subscriptions, renewals, sales mail and record-keeping. I don't remember the name of the first person I hired but I certainly remember the setting. The office had just moved to the Bay Building. There wasn't much furniture other than the three big drafting tables and high stools from Norbert Schaal that were so handy in preparing mail. There was a secretary's small typewriter desk; on its side were emblazoned the initials "HEW" — Hanford Engineering Works, a castoff from the plant that made the nuclear bomb and cost me $13.91, sales tax included. I still have the desk at home.

I was not really ready when I hired the first secretary. Her chair was a wooden orange crate. She did not seem to mind, but neither did she last long. For myself I sat on a wooden box at the typewriter. It seemed more important to get out the next issue of the newsletter than to go searching for a comfortable second-hand chair.

Still looking for help, I left a request with the State Employment Office. Here came a lucky break. The office sent Helen Bertram. She and her husband had recently moved from Tacoma. As she recounted in a letter years afterward: "They gave me a list of three employers to investigate. Luckily, I went to your office first, liked it, and decided to give it a try. Little did I know that the 'tryout' would last 21 years."

Mrs. Bertram fitted in beautifully. She did not want, nor did I need, full-time work. She commuted with her husband, a career man in the U.S. Customs Service, whose office was nearby. She took on more and more tasks that I found I could shake off, handled all the subscription records, prepared lists for sales mail, and kept the accounts. She had my complete trust, and as we shall see in a later incident, she was certainly my "confidential" secretary. In the formality of our informal office, she was always "Mrs. Bertram" and I "Mr. Marple." She remained until her husband retired in 1978. She was an incredible find. It took years before I was equally successful in finding Mike Parks, my successor as editor and publisher.

We remained in the Bay Building for a dozen years. Toward the end I doubt that even a quarter of its space was occupied. Rental income surely could not cover heat, light, taxes, minimum maintenance, and whatever was paid the two elderly women who, each working a half day, ran the building's one elevator from 7 a.m. to 6 p.m. The morning operator, incidentally, was glad to pick up extra change joining my afternoon crew stuffing sales mail in the spring push for *Hobson's Farm Forecast*.

The Garden of Allah gave up in 1956. Warned that the building would soon close, I moved, also in 1956, to the Colman Building, a half-dozen blocks south on First Avenue and up a good half-dozen notches in respectability. The Whitman estate, owner of the Bay Building and the kitty-corner Arcade Building, gave up on the Bay Building and left it cold and empty, a ghost from a time gone by.

In 1974 the building fell to the wrecking ball. Years later with the upgrading of First Avenue there was built on that choice view site a 30-story building, Harbor Steps. The First Avenue level became home to a gift shop, flower shop and art gallery. Higher up the building contained 285 luxury apartments and the 20-room Inn at Harbor Steps. Times change!

CHAPTER THIRTEEN
A 10-Year Perspective

The decade of the 1950s brought perhaps the greatest development of the industrial base of the Pacific Northwest in the long stretch between World War II and the computer era of the 1990s. To tell this story the newsletter took the occasion of its 10th anniversary in May 1959 to issue its first 8-page issue: four pages to highlight the past 10 years, and a second four pages to look at the challenge of the next 10 years. As a starter the newsletter cited "factories that simply did not exist 10 years ago:

"In pulp & paper, there are the new mills of Potlatch Forests at Lewiston, Ida., of Weyerhaeuser at Springfield, Ore., and on Grays Harbor, Scott at Everett, Waldorf near Missoula, Georgia-Pacific at Toledo, Ore., Western Kraft at Albany, Boise Cascade on the Columbia below Pasco. In plywood, 61 new plants have been erected.

"In metals, you see Harvey at The Dalles and Anaconda near Kalispell with the new aluminum smelters. Hanna near Riddle, Ore., is producing nickel. Uranium ore is processed at Lakeview, Ore., and at Ford, Wash. In petroleum, refineries have been built on Puget Sound by General Petroleum, Shell, Texaco, and U.S. Oil & Refining.

"In chemicals, you find sulfuric acid plants at Bunker Hill at Kellogg, Ida., American Smelting & Refining at Tacoma, and Simplot at Pocatello. Factories to make phosphate and fertilizer have been put up by Simplot, Westvaco and Monsanto in the Pocatello area. Phillips-Pacific built the region's first major nitrogen plant at Kennewick. Others have expanded, like Pennsalt at Portland, Borden at Kent, Reichhold at Tacoma, and American-Marietta at Seattle.

"In electronics, a strong new industry has sprung up, paced by Tektronix at Portland and United Control at Seattle. In food processing, southern Idaho has had more new construction than in any 10 years. In less spectacular instances, smaller manufacturers of industrial and consumer products have started up. For an indication of the changing character of Pacific Northwest's basic industries note the chart on page 2." The charts, the first the newsletter published and excruciating to prepare in days before computers, showed consistent 10-year increases in employment except in forest products and agriculture.

Who were big employers in manufacturing? Eight of the top 18 were in forest products. Here are the half-dozen largest:

    Boeing, coming into the jet age, 71,600.
    Weyerhaeuser up nearly 50% in a decade to 13,964.
    Anaconda in Montana and Idaho, 10,120.
    Puget Sound Naval Shipyard, Bremerton, 10,000.
    Crown Zellerbach, Washington and Oregon, 8,071.
    Atomic Energy Commission, Hanford, Wash., 7,972.

Railroads and utilities had big payrolls:

Pacific Telephone, three states, 15,535.
Union Pacific, three states, 10,745.
Northern Pacific, four states, 9,688.
Great Northern, three states, 8,263.
Milwaukee RR, three states, 3,174.

In the second four pages of this 10th anniversary issue the look ahead recognized "the need for industrial growth and diversification." Among likely sources of expansion were consumer goods for the increasing population, raw materials for heavy industry, food processing and "scenery....Scenery can be sold and resold without wearing out. With promotion and construction of new vacation facilities, this region can add millions to its income from the tourist trade."

There were cautions, too. The region had to get away from "the heavy reliance on the cyclical lumber-plywood industry and the dangerous dependence on a single industry like Boeing." It added: "Plywood cannot continue to expand at its present breathtaking pace," a caution that, as we shall see later, could not have been closer to the mark.

That double issue permitted a little bragging, too. Under the heading, "Continuous subscribers for six years or longer," the back page was solid with the names of 207 companies, a diverse who's-who in Pacific Northwest business. That list capped an opening statement that "with almost unbroken succession through 10 years, each issue has had more paid subscribers than the previous issue."

The list of subscribers got a good boost from promotion of this double issue. There was also constant encouragement in the renewal rate, which held close to 90 percent, then and to this day. That's far above magazine renewals, but renewals for a regional letter have to be high because the market is so limited.

Most certainly, however, the newsletter all along could have taken greater promotion. David Pollock, head of the advertising agency of that name, pushed me repeatedly to go on radio with a news program. "Yes, David, I know it would help, but if I take on one more task they'll be carrying me out in a pine box."

Later, usually pushed by a subscriber, I did some speaking to business groups, but reluctantly because of the time required for preparation. In turning down a request to speak to an Aberdeen group, I wrote that I would do "neither the audience nor myself any good unless I could prepare adequately." Today Mike Parks, with the deftness of an old pro, has become easily the best known speaker on the Pacific Northwest economy, a great plus for the audience and the newsletter.

Chapter Fourteen
Walker's Weekly Newsletter

One day a well-dressed man, perhaps in his late 40s, carrying a heavy satchel, came to the newsletter office in the Bay Building. I knew he was a stranger because he followed the hallway to the front door of the office instead of taking the shortcut through the inside room that we used for mailing and supplies. He handed me his card: Bryce Reynolds, vice-president of Walker's Manual, Inc. He was up from San Francisco to call on banks, stock brokers and corporate treasurers, selling *Walker's Manual of Pacific Coast Securities*. His company recognized a growing interest in publicly held stocks of Pacific Northwest companies and wanted to expand here. He had picked up my name as he made his rounds. He little knew, and I could never have guessed, that his call would open up a whole new field of reporting in the newsletter.

Walker's Manual, long established, carried financial details on every publicly held West Coast company. It might be regarded as the *Standard & Poor's* for the West. The two or three pages it devoted to each company I had already found in the public library as a great resource. Bryce's proposal was simple: he would promote the *Manual* by mail from San Francisco; may he leave a copy with me for any interested person to examine? Certainly, yes!

Reynolds left the fat current issue, and year after year sent a new issue. Nobody ever came to examine the *Manual*, but I certainly used it and was grateful for the handout. More important, however, was the manual's companion publication that I had not heard of, *Walker's Weekly Newsletter*. Also published in San Francisco it carried up-to-the-minute information on companies that were included on an annual basis in the *Manual*. In a few days Joe Taylor, editor of Walker's newsletter, wrote. Would I send him news from time to time on Pacific Northwest companies? Yes, glad to have another customer.

Walker's Weekly Newsletter, printed on distinctive pumpkin-colored paper, reported each issue in detail on four or five companies of interest to investors. Each company account opened with narrative — what's new on products, markets, revenues, earnings, finances, key personnel, etc. The back of that sheet carried the company's financials in tabular form — sales, earnings, balance sheet, etc., with comparison for recent years and quarters.

Taylor put together the tabular material, a tedious typewriter task that I was glad to skip. What he wanted from me was the narrative, whatever the company would loosen up to say, solid information, no forecasting. That was the style of reporting I liked. Taylor pushed me for about one company a month, but the number varied with the flow of news. As a guide as to what Walker's wanted, Taylor's boss, Lewis B. Reynolds, president and publisher, wrote that my first story (on Pacific Car and Foundry) "was a honey...just the kind of thing we like to have — full of real, honest-to-god exclusive news, and a lot of good basic dope besides."

That was encouraging, but Walker's was putting a further squeeze on my time. For its stories I went out to a company to talk to as high an official as I could get, often the president or financial vice-president; Walker's letter was respected for its investor following. For me the squeeze could not have come at a worse time. Soon I'd be deep into writing the history of the National Bank of Commerce of Seattle — interviews, library work, and then the writing, as I shall soon recount.

Somehow I had to find time for Walker's between issues of my newsletter and reporting for *Business Week* and tradepapers. In the two-week cycle of the newsletter I'd complete writing an issue by Monday evening, mail on Tuesday, send out sales mail on Wednesday, and have the rest of that week clear for other publications. At this point I'd dig in on the bank history until I had to break off to begin reporting for the next issue of the newsletter. How, I asked myself, can I squeeze more time for the bank history that held me down like lead weights on a diver's suit?

That's where *Walker's Weekly Newsletter* came in. Surely, out of a company interview and reporting for Walker's there must be material I could use in my own newsletter; I had more space for narrative than *Walker's*, could pull in more background for perspective, and could focus solely on the Pacific Northwest. Using this material, already in hand, would save a day or two of reporting on some other topic for the next issue.

I tried putting this investor information into a company profile for the middle two pages of the newsletter. To my surprise these profiles drew more comment than almost anything else I wrote about. Thus began investment reports on companies in Seattle, Portland, Boise, Spokane and cities in between. That series continues to this day, expanded and more frequent under Mike Park's editorship.

Company officials welcomed the attention, I found. The president of Boise Cascade, in Seattle on other business, sought me out one afternoon for a long interview in the corner of an empty meeting room at the Washington Athletic Club. Thanks to the day that Bryce Reynolds walked into my office I caught on to the growing interest of investors in Pacific Northwest stocks. Moreover, the economy of this region was creating investors looking for ways to participate in the growth they saw all about them.

Joe Taylor and I recognized that his letter and mine differed enough in content and audience so that there was no real conflict. However, I told him that if he suggested a company for me to cover he should run the story first. And vice versa if I originated the story. We understood each other; there was never a problem.

By now I also had a little money to invest and carefully looked over companies in this region. I made the self-imposed rule: from the time I started working on a company profile until two weeks after my newsletter carried that story, I neither buy nor sell that stock. I cannot recall a time when I did not wait at least a month. That rule remains with the newsletter to this day.

I wrote for *Walker's Weekly Newsletter* for 15 years, one of my better accounts. But in 1974, that newsletter, after passing through two ownerships, died in the hard times that hit stock brokers and investors. The *Manual*, to which I did not contribute, continues to this day.

CHAPTER FIFTEEN
Rough News in Mining *and* Plywood

Sometimes background information combined with on-the-scene reporting can pull from an obscure event a story of national significance. Witness two examples: how a mining enterprise faded and how the plywood industry went south.

When the mining town of Kellogg in the mountains of northern Idaho was racked by a strike that ran on week after week I put other things aside and drove over to talk to the company and the union and learn the impact on the town itself. The issues were more than local. The strike was against Bunker Hill Co., the second largest U.S. producer of lead, a major producer of zinc, and the town's only reason for existence. But lead and zinc were now in worldwide overproduction. Imports were rising. The Mine, Mill & Smelter Union, of admitted left-wing leadership, tried to hold to the standards reached in a lusher time.

The newsletter told the story in the middle two pages under the headline, "Special Report: A town caught in the showdown with a left-wing union." The two sides hung tough in a clash such as sweeps over an industry when its glory days live only in memory. The paychecks of nearly half the residents of the entire county came from Bunker Hill. The town bled.

The strike came at a historic turn. The mining and smelting of lead and zinc in the Pacific Northwest was on a long downslide. Ore came now from deeper mines, more costly to bring up. Competition from offshore ore kept prices down, and before long, environmental constraints bit hard. After the strike Bunker Hill closed its smelter and tore down the great brick chimney whose plume once signaled prosperity but now was doomed for its pollution. Today tourism is the town's mainstay, history and skiing are the attractions, and the townspeople worry over lead that leaches from mine tailings and pollutes the stream flowing through the town.

The visit to Kellogg and that story brought a letter from C.E. Schwab, the Bunker Hill president: "I want to express my appreciation for your visiting Kellogg during our strike and to also extend my compliments for a very factual job of reporting in contrast to the article that appeared in Time Magazine. Your write-up, which subsequently also became a story in Business Week, very thoroughly explained the problems in a grim situation."

The plywood story stemmed from two separate news releases. Each was intended as just a mill announcement, but as sometimes happens the releases ignored the larger story that lay silent between the lines.

Such was the case with two releases in 1963, each announcing construction of a plywood plant presumed to be of trifling concern beyond two mill towns. But the announcements contained something I had been watching for. I seized them as the newspeg for a story headlined, "Plywood Manufacturing Moves into the South - a Special Report." I called it a "special report" because it was important enough to fill the middle two pages, and I needed to give a little aura to a story that a reader might otherwise grumble: "Why does this guy write so much on a topic that I don't care about?"

What gave this news its significance was the unstated background. For most of the century the nation's softwood plywood was made from old-growth Douglas fir in the Pacific Northwest and from old-growth Douglas fir logs. In time, the newsletter recounted, the industry reached out for smaller, lower-grade logs for sheathing — rough but sturdy plywood panels used as underlayment of floors and walls, soon accounting for half of all softwood plywood.

Markets nationwide called for more. That put pressure on raw material. Laboratory research earlier found ways to make plywood from other species such as hemlock and larch. That helped a bit, but for some time federal and private research was directed to a more extensive raw material, Montana pine, a resinous wood that required new technology in drying and gluing. Leaders in the industry pushed this research in the recognition that the technique for Montana would apply to the resinous but much more abundant southern pine and thus would open the way for the industry to move into the South.

That was the unstated significance in the announcements that Georgia-Pacific would build a plywood plant in Arkansas and U.S. Plywood in Texas. The implications for the Pacific Northwest, the newsletter said, were as unmistakable as they were unpalatable.

Our checking with leaders in plywood and with manufacturers of their machinery established beyond question: Mills in the South, using the new process, would start with the economies of the most efficient machinery and plant design in contrast to older mills of the Pacific NW. More important, the South had lower freight costs to markets of the East and South and lower-cost raw material (southern pine was growing faster than it was being harvested). A leader in the southern forest industry forecast that within five years output of southern plywood would equal 30 percent of the output of mills in the West.

Subsequent cutbacks in Washington and Oregon, the newsletter warned, would hurt. Plywood had been one of the great growth industries of the Pacific NW, output up five-fold in 14 years. While employment in Oregon's logging and sawmills tumbled in a decade from 68,600 to 37,800, employment in plywood rose in the same decade from 10,200 to 23,900.

Market promotion developed for Pacific Northwest plywood now carried into the South. "Southern producers are insistent that their plywood go to market as a quality product," the newsletter reported. "Last week the southern committee working on standards agreed to meet grade requirements of Douglas Fir Plywood Assn. As a result a good share of new southern plywood mills will join DFPA to obtain its grade-testing and labeling service. In turn, DFPA will remove 'Douglas fir' from its name and will establish new testing and other technical facilities in the South."

Such was the story behind the routine announcement of two new mills. The rest is history. By the late 1990s two-thirds of the nation's plywood came from the South. The number of plywood mills in Oregon, Washington, Montana and Idaho fell from 141 at the peak in the 1960s to 43 in 1996; most of those remaining concentrate on high-priced sanded panels best made from Douglas fir.

The migration of plywood to the South was as overwhelming as the migration of the New England textile mills to the South early in this century. The newsletter's summary drew this note from C.W. Lewis Jr. of the Louisiana Forestry Association: "Your observations [on southern pine plywood] are astute and, coming from a reliable West Coast source, take on added significance."

The Douglas Fir Plywood Association, some of whose biggest members led the way to the South, broadened its name to American Plywood Association. Its headquarters and principal research laboratories remain in Tacoma, but it has a full-scale regional office in Georgia and five marketing offices in Europe and Japan. Because many of its members expanded into other forms of glued wood — oriented strand board, glulam lumber and wood I-joists — the association extended its quality control and grade marking to those products also and recently changed its name to APA-The Engineered Wood Association.

Chapter Sixteen
How to Take a Month Off

It took a trip to Turkey, nearly 20 years after the start of the newsletter, for me to find what subscribers liked most. The trip was a long time coming. Dot and I had talked of a vacation in Austria, our first in Europe and of special interest to Dot for music. But my niece Lisa Bentley and her husband, living in Ankara and speaking Turkish, interposed. Come visit us, they urged: "We can show you finer examples of Greek architecture and sculpture than you can find in Greece, and we can take you places you would not visit on your own." Very compelling!

There was another prod. Rotary International was holding its 1967 convention in late May on the French Mediterranean at Nice. The Seattle Rotary Club, of which I was a member, was chartering a plane to fly members and spouses directly to Nice and return four weeks later from London. Tempting! But what would happen to the newsletter, the product of one man and a part-time secretary? I had learned that I could skip one issue for vacation, but I dared not shut the whole business down for four weeks.

Intent on making the trip, I took a cue from the 10-year anniversary issue, now almost forgotten, and worked out this schedule: I completed the current issue and left it for Mrs. Bertram to mail. At the bottom of that issue I stuck the note: "Vacation. No issue June 14." I had done that before and nobody objected. That would take care of the first two weeks away. For the second two weeks I wrote a special number that I regarded as just a thumb-sucker and left for Mrs. Bertram to put out.

That special issue broke from the pattern of the newsletter. Instead of reporting immediate developments it stood back and offered perspective on the forces shaping the region. Under the headline, "Profile of the Economy," it focused on "three basic industries that more than any others pull dollars into the Pacific Northwest and nourish the economy — forest products, aerospace and agriculture. Expansion in the decade ahead will rest heavily on those industries. Even more important, each is entering a period of long-term stability unmatched in the history of the region."

In forest products, for decades "lumber and shingles were the main products, and from the earliest days mills were plagued by overproduction and abrupt swings between feast and famine. But the industry has broadened into pulp, paper, plywood, particleboard, chemicals and prefabricated parts; it is not just larger, it is more soundly based."

The record was impressive — seven new pulp & paper mills, 61 new plywood mills, major additions in light metals and chemicals, a cluster of oil refineries, and in southern Idaho unparalleled expansion in food processing.

For perspective, employment in forest products, responding to the postwar housing boom, had reached an all-time high in 1951 of 92,400 in Oregon and 75,800 in Washington. That high has not been touched in the succeeding half-century. In Idaho and Montana the forest industry for the first time employed more people than traditional mining and metals.

Charts showed how "the face of manufacturing is changing." The biggest gains in employment were not in basic manufacturing but in secondary or diversified industry. The aerospace industry, "with employment now pushing toward 96,000, provides the explosive factor in today's economy — and the chills for those who judge this industry only from roller-coaster swings of earlier years." Boeing's strength long-term, the 1967 profile continued, "lies in its organization — the ability to tackle extremely complex jobs; to research, design, test and manufacture; and above all to finance and sell."

Agriculture, the profile continued, "will expand in the next decade. Two simple reasons: there are more mouths to feed, in the U.S. and the world, and every year thousands of productive acres are lost in the relentless spread of cities, factories and freeways...in California, the nation's No. 1 agricultural state."

Irrigation, especially in the Columbia Basin, will pull more dollars from the soil, and "limitations on wheat, the Pacific NW's most important crop, will give way to incentives for greater production...Expansion in agriculture will bring parallel expansion in food processing — canning, freezing and dehydration for distant markets. Jobs created in processing will help replace those lost on the farm through mechanization."

When I left for Turkey I was uneasy with this special issue. The perspective, the conclusions, seemed inescapable, but this was a marked departure for the newsletter, possible only after several of years of a reporter's prodding into every corner of the economy.

When I returned a month later I was staggered to learn of the response — more requests for extra copies than ever before; so many, in fact, that we ordered a rerun of the entire issue, the first time that was ever done. Many subscribers asked for 10 or 20 copies to mail to customers, suppliers, and head offices in the Midwest and East. The international department of Seattle-First National Bank alone asked for 300 copies. A subscriber in Tokyo with ties to the Pacific Northwest put in his order, and so did many others. We were glad to provide reprints without charge.

By the end of 1967 the subscription list touched a new high, 2,026. The newsletter has continued to this day a special year-end issue of perspective and outlook. Sometimes that issue is a double number, eight pages, illustrated in recent years with charts. It always brings calls for extra copies, and it remains a great source of new subscribers.

Chapter Seventeen
A Bank and Its Story

Early in the 1960s Maxwell Carlson, president of the National Bank of Commerce in Seattle, asked me to come up to his office. Would I write the bank's history? He had before him a small volume, around 140 pages, that a Minneapolis bank had just published. This was suggestive, but he was thinking of something broader. Because the National Bank of Commerce was founded in 1889, the year Washington become a state, he wanted to tell the story of the bank in the context of the state's first 75 years. Mr. Carlson went a step further. The men (there were then no women at the top) who had guided the bank through its early years were retired or soon would be. They were disappearing. He wanted to capture their part of history before it became lost.

The project was intriguing. The bank, commonly called NBofC, was second largest in the state. Competition with the leader, Seattle-First National Bank, was intense. The two institutions fought for commercial and consumer accounts, and as they pushed into eastern Washington fought to buy local banks and convert them into branches. The history Mr. Carlson had in mind would include also Marine Bancorporation, the bank's holding company that the late Andrew Price founded in the heady 1920s.

Maxwell Carlson — he was always "Mr. Carlson" to me and I think to almost all the staff — had always seemed distant, almost austere. His title as president meant that he was very much the chief executive officer years before that designation came into general play. I don't recall that I ever went to him for news of banking; when I needed to, I worked with officers just under him. But he knew me of course through the newsletter.

Time for the history was growing short. The 75th anniversaries of the bank and the state lay just ahead. As we talked, Mr. Carlson made clear that I'd have a free hand. I'd have said no immediately if the book was to be about just the bank. But the concept of tying the history of the bank to that of the state had more appeal.

I asked for time to think it over. There was no discussion of compensation. Mr. Carlson assigned the project to Andrew Price Jr., vice-president, son of Marine's founder, and "Andy" to everybody. I knew he would be pleasant to work with.

On and off through the next three or four weeks Andy and I talked. I did not see how I could find time to take this on. I gave him the names and qualifications of two or three other writers in town. But no, he kept coming back to me as though Mr. Carlson had said I was the man he wanted. An essential part of the book would be the story of Marine Bancorporation, going back to the 1920s. For this the bank already had called in Bruce H. Olson from the faculty of the University of Washington School of Business Administration for a summer of research and writing.

Reluctantly, I said yes. I began taping interviews with older bank officers, some present, some retired. This of course would become raw material for the bank history and would become a packet for the bank's archives.

The founder of the bank, Robert R. Spencer, was long since dead, but I picked up his trail in letters, some written even before he came to Seattle. Spencer was cashier, and that meant manager, of a small bank in Iowa City, Iowa. The Northern Pacific Railway had just reached Puget Sound and opened a world of excitement and opportunity. Spencer, restless but with the caution of a banker, took the railroad west intent on establishing a bank. His letters tell of the bustle he found in the land just opening up and of the beginning of a bank that grew bigger than he had ever anticipated.

I worked on the history whenever I could steal time from the newsletter, from assignments by *Business Week* that included an occasional cover story, and from tradepaper reporting. Professor Olson became so fascinated with Marine Bancorporation that his research report ran longer than was planned for the entire book. His style of writing differed, too, so I ended up rewriting and condensing his important segment.

With luck on my work schedule I might have two or three days at a stretch on the bank story. Then I'd break off to get the next issue of the newsletter out. The weeks were long, and Saturday a full workday. When my wife Dot and I were late for a Saturday evening game of bridge with our neighbors, Les and Barbara Ackley, Les would growl: "When are you going to finish that damn bank story?" Though Dot was not well, no one could guess that before the book was published Les and Dot would die a day apart, and a year later Barbara and I would marry.

The book, *The National Bank of Commerce of Seattle*, subtitled "Territorial to Worldwide Banking in Eighty Years," came out in 1972. It was illustrated by the Seattle artist Nicholas T. Kritikos, and published by Pacific Books, Palo Alto, California. Distribution was by the bank, and before long copies became a collector's item.

I was paid $5,500, a figure that Andy Price voluntarily raised above our informal agreement. The research and writing took far more time than I had anticipated. I never told Andy that the timesheet which a self-employed person keeps as a constant prod showed I earned less, per hour, from the book than I paid my part-time secretary.

There is a sequel to the book and to Mr. Carlson's retirement in 1971 at age 65. Marine Bancorporation, launched in 1927, was one of the oldest bank holding companies in the U.S. The elder Andrew Price was credited with coining the term "bancorporation" for a company that brought together a number of banks under common ownership. He began by buying banks in outlying cities. Then he bought the National Bank of Commerce in Seattle and brought his outlying banks in to function as branches. Marine added other subsidiaries. It raised money by selling its own stock, usually in small amounts to uninitiated investors. That was the style of Wall Street in the late '20s. There was no Securities and Exchange Commission to slow him down. Marine sold stock like hamburgers at McDonald's. At the peak Marine had 6,000 stockholders, far more than any of the much larger banks in Seattle or Portland. In 1948 Mr. Carlson became president of National Bank of Commerce, at 42 one of the youngest bank presidents in America. He built with skill and caution and financed growth entirely out of earnings, the only billion-dollar West Coast bank to do so. He set up an international department with offices in London, New York and Hong Kong. He proudly relied on the bank's own reserves against losses rather than turn to the Federal Reserve for help. In a little more than the 21 years of his presidency, the bank's deposits rose nearly four-fold to top $1 billion.

But large investors shied away from the stock. To meet criticism Marine extended voting rights from the two percent of its shares held by the founders to the 98 percent held by the public. Even so, the stock dragged in comparison with other banks. A table I worked out ever so laboriously for the newsletter in 1973 showed that Marine's shares, alone of the statewide banks in Seattle and Portland, traded over-the-counter below book value, sometimes at not much more than half of book value. "Loaded with value and no way to get it out," the newsletter reported in the quip of a veteran stock broker.

To Mr. Carlson the situation was intolerable. By now he had retired as president but continued as a director. He was disappointed in his successor, chosen from within the bank, and earnings were down. One evening he called me at home. He knew I had tried to see him that afternoon for the story I was preparing on the bank. I gave him two chances to say I would go to his office, but, no, he wanted to come to mine. I was flabbergasted! I seldom drew a visitor, and never one of such consequence.

"The next morning he came in," my typed notes read, "tall and a little Lincolnesque in his simplicity and durability and integrity. His temples are now gray but his hair is still essentially black [age 67]. He carries a big pocket watch at the end of a heavy gold chain across his vest. I introduced him to my secretary, Mrs. Bertram. He asked at once: 'Is she your *confidential* secretary?' I said yes, she had been with me for 12 or 15 years. He repeated with stress: 'Is she your *confidential* secretary?' I assured him again and he sat down by the big window that almost filled one end of a long, narrow, dark room, and began to talk. He emphasized that he was talking to me as the man who had done the bank history and I'd be writing for some time yet and might need the background. He stressed that he was not talking to Marple as editor of the newsletter. That put me in a hard spot; as a basic rule I will not take anything off the record, but in this case I figured OK." Mrs. Bertram sensed the tenseness and left.

Then, my notes continued, he began to tell me of the changes since his retirement. Sixteen months ago Andrew Price Jr. resigned from both Marine and the bank and went on vacation, and Robert Faragher, who had moved up as president of the bank, was in the Orient. So Mr. Carlson stepped in to fill the void. He formed an ad hoc committee of directors to find a new president with "superior leadership." He set up another committee on the bank's name. "Marine" had served its purpose and was confused with Marine Midland in New York, and "National Bank of Commerce" was certainly cumbersome.

The committee looking for a president interviewed many people, but the members became discouraged and could not see when they would finish. The 90 days Carlson gave them became 16 months. Mr. Carlson emphasized, "We were not just going to sit and wait. There is no excuse for the poor earnings of last year, the poorest of any large bank on the West Coast except the Bank of California," which he dismissed for a new direction it was taking in real estate investments. Mr. Carlson also pushed the reorganization of subsidiaries. A vice-president who sometimes picked me up at my bus stop on the way to work protested that though Mr. Carlson was no longer president, "he will not let go."

When I mentioned to Mr. Carlson that I was told that morning that the international banking department had earned "substantial profits," he broke in: "Omit the adjective." At another point he said: "We have a problem in international banking....I blew the whistle on international banking. I blew the whistle on the management of NBofC."

Finally, under Mr. Carlson's prodding, the bank got a new president, G. Robert Truex Jr., pulled out of Bank of America, where he was executive vice-president. Mr. Carlson had given Truex's name to the ad hoc committee. "Truex had called on us and I called on him in New York when he was with Irving Trust." Mr. Carlson thoroughly enjoyed those visits. He did not have sports or outside activities to chit-chat about so they talked business and details. Truex previously told me that he came to dread those meetings because of the penetrating questions. Truex always saw to it that he had two associates with him; if he couldn't answer a Carlson question he would point to an associate who could.

When Mr. Carlson came into my office that morning he laid on the broad oak windowsill a packet of eight or ten stapled sheets. As he got up to go, after an hour and a half, he said he would leave that material for me to read, strictly in confidence. He added that Ralph Stowell, his close associate and fellow director, would be horrified if he knew Mr. Carlson had given the material to me.

The material he left included letters to the board and others. My notes read: "They were critical, some highly critical, and pointed out weak spots that had to be corrected. I did not have time to read them until later in the day and for the first time wished I had a key to lock my desk at night. The papers were plain dynamite — if they got in the hands of an unkind newspaper. The next morning I returned the papers to Mr. Carlson, expressed appreciation for his confidence, and reassured him that I had made no copies, took no notes. I probably should have jotted down at least the dates of directors' meetings to the minutes of which Mr. Carlson attached his letters.

I have never before revealed Mr. Carlson's visit. I remained puzzled why he came to me. He talked at length of problems in the London office, and I felt that he wanted me to be ready when those problems burst open, which they never did. But he was a troubled man. I should have asked questions to clear up matters as he spoke, but this was his story; it was not for publication, and I didn't feel that I should break in.

Six years later on the occasion when Mike Parks became editor of the newsletter, Maxwell Carlson wrote me a kind word:

"Over the years your insight of business in its broadest aspects has been remarkable, and I have admired particularly your capacity to identify the myriad of nuances which others find difficult to sense and relate properly.

"As we retire the most satisfying legacy we can leave is our reputation of competence and integrity. Your reputation in your particular field of endeavor is well established and deserves to be properly recognized."

Mr. Carlson retired to his summer home on Hood Canal and several years later died of cancer, an illness that had troubled him when he was still bank president. I regret that I did not go to visit him in his closing months.

Under Truex's leadership, the bank completed the turnaround that Mr. Carlson had pushed so hard. As the newsletter reported, in 30 days the price of its stock rose 23 percent, the sharpest gain of any Pacific Coast bank. Mr. Carlson himself showed his confidence by buying 1,000 shares, adding to what must have been substantial earlier holdings.

Truex built vigorously. He gave the bank an easily recognized name, Rainier. In time as part of an irrepressible trend toward regionwide and then nationwide banking, Rainier merged into Security Pacific of Los Angeles, and Truex, in poor health, retired.

Later Security Pacific merged into Bank of America, which already had acquired Seattle-First National (Seafirst). In turn, Seafirst took over Rainier's offices and branches and wiped out Rainier's name. At that time, if you drove down Second Avenue in Seattle, you would come at Spring Street to the five-story building to which Maxwell Carlson had added a floor for the bank's expanding headquarters. Overhead, sticking out on the corner of the building, hung the identification: "Seafirst Bank." There could have been no greater humiliation for Maxwell Carlson, who spent his career in vigorous and respectful competition with Seafirst. He did not live to see the final blow — his bank and his own office taken over by the enemy.

Investors who bought stock in Pacific Northwest banks did well. As the region grew, its banks grew. They earned well, paid some dividends in cash, plowed most of their earnings back for growth, and gave their stockholders additional shares to match the earnings plowed back.

Here's a suggestion of the return to stockholders: in 1974 I bought 225 shares of Marine Bancorporation (holding company of National Bank of Commerce) for $5,540. For a time my stock was under water — worth less than I had paid for it. Then earnings improved. Marine became Rainier Bank. Rainier issued a stock dividend that doubled the number of shares I held. Eight years of growth brought another doubling. In time, Security Pacific in Los Angeles bought Rainier and gave me Security Pacific stock. Five years passed and Bank of America bought Security Pacific and gave me Bank of America stock. Five years further along Bank of America split its stock two for one — another doubling in the shares I held. Bank of America shares rose to a new high in July 1998. At that point, stock that had cost me $5,540 had a market value of $206,000. This does not include annual cash dividends.

For earlier investors, notably bank founders, the buildup was much greater and suggests how some of today's family fortunes arose. The 1,000 shares that Maxwell Carlson added in 1973 for $18,875 would, if held into 1998, have become Bank of America stock with market value of $915,000 paying cash dividends of $12,600 a year. Microsoft was not the first skyrocket.

Chapter Eighteen
Paccar Makes the News

I had long wanted to do a profile on Paccar, the builder of heavy-duty Kenworth and Peterbilt trucks. Though the company's employment in 1971 was far short of Boeing's, Paccar stood as the second largest manufacturer in the Seattle area and provided important diversification. The company was one of the few in the Pacific Northwest ranked in *Fortune*'s 500.

Once known as Pacific Car and Foundry and privately held, it had some 4,000 stockholders across the country and even overseas. But management remained uneasy talking to outsiders in the transition from a little-known regional company to a manufacturer selling worldwide. It had no vice-president for public relations and turned aside reporters and stock brokers asking questions.

The company's very aloofness made it a bigger target for me. As with many companies I dropped into a file folder bits and pieces of news that were of no use at the moment but might some time help on background. The day would come, I figured, when I'd have enough material, enough understanding, to weave a full-scale meaningful report. A part of that report would be the simple statement that the story was done over the company's dead body — i.e., it refused to talk.

Paccar built Kenworth trucks in Seattle, Kansas City, Montreal, Mexico and Vancouver, B.C. It expanded with purchase of the competing Peterbilt line of trucks, built at Newark, California, and Nashville, Tennessee. It built railroad freight cars at Renton, on the edge of Seattle, and winches, hoists, forgings and other specialty items. Its structural steel division in Seattle fabricated (at a loss) the exterior load-bearing panels for the 100-story World Trade Center in New

York. It employed 7,800, nearly half in the Seattle area. An intriguing company!

Among bits in the file folder were typed notes of a conversation I had had some years earlier with Thomas F. Gleed, formerly president of Seafirst Bank, now a director of Paccar. When Paul Pigott bought control of the company, awash in red ink in 1934, a Depression year, Gleed asked: "What are you buying that rust pile for?" Pigott replied: "Because I think that with local management we can make the preferred stock [which investors had accepted in Depression-era restructuring] worth something and we can build an industry and payroll the Northwest needs."

Another note recalled the casual comment of a top officer during a break at a trade conference: "We tackle the giants of American industry." The giants in truck-building included General Motors, Ford, International Harvester and White. Against that competition Paccar held 12 percent of U.S. registrations of new heavy-duty trucks. [That percentage of a much bigger market nearly doubled by the late 1990s.]

The file turned up other bits, such as insight from a Peterbilt distributor whom I looked in on now and then for McFadden's *Trucking* letter.

The picture was filling in, but I lacked a news peg — a development that would open the story. One day that news peg popped up. Paccar filed with the Securities and Exchange Commission for a public offering of $15 million in 25-year debentures. The offering, mainly to pay down bank loans, was insignificant by itself and brought Paccar's total debt to only $21 million, far less than stockholder equity of $126 million ($45.90 a common share). The prospectus for an offering of bonds is sketchy at best, quite unlike the detailed prospectus for an offering of stock, but it was newspeg enough for a story.

I was well into the writing when I caught myself and said: "Wait a minute, Marple. These are decent people, and long a subscriber. You ought at least have the courtesy to let them know that you will have their story in the next issue." I phoned the secretary of Charles Pigott, who had succeeded his father, Paul, as president and chief executive. Hardly an hour later a call came back: "Mr. Pigott will be glad to see you." I was flabbergasted.

In the interview Mr. Pigott could not have been more considerate. The next week the newsletter devoted the two center pages to Paccar. It did not quote anyone except Mr. Pigott's concession that the company did maintain "a low profile." But I had the important detail and knew I was on the right track for the first coherent account of how the company began, where growth was taking it, and how investors had fared. After the issue came out, several stock analysts and reporters asked how I ever got in. I could only smile.

Paccar's sale of debentures was the only public offering of any kind that the company ever made. Instead of selling stock it financed growth out of earnings and rewarded its shareholders with dividends in stock as well as cash. The Pigott family, then and now, remained the largest stockholders, but shares were also spread among employees through payroll deduction. As employees retired or died their shares often came on the market. The number of shareholders increased from 270 in 1950 to 4,000 in 1971, when the newsletter's story appeared.

As the newsletter reported, the company's sales, earnings and net worth rose nearly four-fold in the previous decade. "Cash dividends get about 20 percent of profits; the rest goes back into the business. Shares have been split repeatedly; a person holding 100 shares in 1945 would have an unbelievable 29,552" in 1971.

Paccar has remained an attractive investment. As an example, my wife Barbara bought 50 shares in 1971 for a total of $2,925. When she died 21 years later, those 50 shares had become 660 with market value of $34,000.

There is a sequel. Several years after the newsletter's profile, Charles Pigott wrote generously of our year-end outlook: "I want to compliment you on your accuracy, perspective, and completeness."

A little later Barry Provorse, whose company, Documentary Book Publishers, has handled a number of company histories, asked if I would write the history of Paccar. I had just retired from the newsletter and had some free time. Provorse and I sat down with Charles Pigott to go over what he had in mind. It was already May, and he wanted a book for distribution at Christmas. That would require delving into company records, interviewing here and outside the company, and some travel. The book that I visualized could not be researched, written and printed in that time. I had to say, no, thanks. Another writer took on the job, the book came out on schedule, and the company was pleased, so much so that it recently ordered a reprint. But that was not the book I'd have written, and I thought it lacked the insight of a reporter who had followed the company for years.

In 1997 Charles Pigott retired and was succeeded by his son Mark C. Pigott, the fourth generation to head the company. By that time Paccar had added plants in England, Holland and Australia, and built nearly 25 percent of all heavy-duty trucks sold in the U.S. Its biggest rival was Freightliner in Portland, which Paccar once tried to buy. But the U.S. antitrust people said no, and Freightliner was acquired instead by the German manufacturer Daimler-Benz. Paccar's stock continues to reward patient investors with stock dividends and stock splits, one of the great investments in the Pacific Northwest.

Chapter Nineteen
All Aboard!

The importance of railroads in the economy a century ago, or even a half-century, is hard to recognize today when airlines and truck lines are so prominent. The completion of the Northern Pacific into Tacoma in 1888 broke the barrier of desert and mountain. Soon other lines came — the Great Northern, the Milwaukee, the Union Pacific, the Southern Pacific, and countless service branches to pick up wheat and lumber, branches later abandoned.

The network of rails opened this country as nothing else could. That interminable walk of first settlers, a thousand miles and more on the Oregon Trail, one step after the other, in dust and sweat, by women and men, oxen and horses, was now only history. The new railroads made an easy approach for settlers and visitors, and for goods moving in both directions.

Freight rates became a touchy subject because the cost of toting the products of farms and factories can open, or close, distant markets. Frozen peas, corn and green beans, important products of the Pacific Northwest, have to absorb the cost of eastbound freight in competition with Minnesota and Wisconsin in reaching the populous eastern markets. Aluminum smelters got their start in Washington, Oregon and Montana because electric power, their big cost, was cheap enough to offset freight to the East. But the sword cut both ways. Simplot, the leader in Idaho potatoes, started a trend by building a french-fry plant in North Dakota to serve markets too costly to reach from Idaho.

Rate-making for years was in the hands of the Interstate Commerce Commission (abolished not too long ago) and state agencies. Rates became Byzantine in their complexity. In reporting the "long-expected showdown on revision of the railroad freight rate structure of the West," the newsletter cautioned in 1953: "Traffic men in the Pacific NW regard the ICC move as the most important in years. For at stake is not just a new set of rates but the manner of rate-making itself. If the ICC held strictly to a mileage basis for all rates, NW manufacturers were barred from dickering for special, lower rates that take into account the long haul to bring in raw materials and to ship NW products to major markets."

Favors and penalties in those days became ingrained all through the system. As an instance, the newsletter reported a fight over preferential treatment for eastern competitors shipping into the West. A Chicago manufacturer was allowed three stops in transit for partial unloading, say at Los Angeles, San Francisco and Portland, and paid the cheaper carload rate. Northwest Metal Products, Kent, Washington, was allowed only one stop in transit and for the additional stops had to pay the higher rate for less-than-carload shipments. A small matter, but sometimes critical. While this case was headed to the ICC, rate experts of the transcontinental rail lines in Chicago worked it over preparatory to making one-stop the basic rule.

Freeways and heavy-duty trucks brought big changes to railroads. Paccar gave up building railroad refrigerator cars to concentrate on its trucks, made especially powerful for mountain highways. Gradually trucks bit off hauls that once were a railroad monopoly. The flexibility of movement by truck contributed to the buildup of smaller distribution centers such as at Missoula, Spokane and Eugene.

Railroads, in turn, put more muscle into fast, efficient moving of bulk commodities, notably grain and coal, often carried in unit trains. Midwest corn moves by trainload to dockside elevators on Puget Sound and the lower Columbia River.

Pacific Coast ports fight for container cargoes in intermodal shipping — the fast handling by ship, truck and rail of goods moving between Asia and the Midwest. The stickiest part is surface congestion as trucks trundle ocean containers between ship and rail.

A half century ago railroads carried most of the people traveling any distance for business or pleasure. Railroad stations bustled with people coming or going or meeting the trains. Passenger trains were a part of routine life.

In days of steam engines, railroads regarded passenger trains as money losers, but they advertised for passengers to build prestige. For years Northern Pacific was "the route of the great baked potato," a boost for its excellent dining-car fare. The Union Pacific "served 11 western states with the finest in travel comfort and dependable freight service." The Milwaukee Road touted its electrified route. Milwaukee was the last of the transcontinental lines to reach Puget Sound — and went out of business, bankrupt.

The comfortable passenger service between Portland and Seattle seems today almost a curiosity. Of the half-dozen passenger trains a day on this 186-mile run, one left each city around 11 p.m. with sleeping cars. Passengers would board a sleeping car in the late evening, undress for a night in a comfortable berth, arrive in the other city around 6 a.m., and have until 7:30 or so to shave, dress and leave for breakfast and work. That leisurely travel lost out to superhighways and automobiles.

In transporting mail, railroads did a superb job — between cities and towns and across the country. They hauled everybody's mail and linked thousands of towns now stranded in the cutback of passenger service. Every passenger train crossing the West had one or more mail cars just behind the locomotive. At every stop the train dropped off and took on canvas sacks of mail.

City post offices scheduled their letter carriers to the arrival of trains. When I moved to the Bay Building there were four deliveries a day; incredible! The heaviest delivery came early, around 8:30 a.m. The second, around 11 a.m., was important for the mail brought to town that morning by the transcontinental trains arriving from the East around 7 to 8 a.m. The Post Office quickly sorted this incoming mail for letter carriers to deliver in their second round. Before the days of airlines, all business communications from any distance came by rail, except only for the few matters important enough to telegraph.

The third delivery came right after lunch, and a final cleanup around 2:30, usually not much in that and indeed, it was the first the Post Office cut off. Between each delivery the carrier hopped a bus back to the postal distribution center near the rail depots. In time we were down to one delivery a day, and by then most of the mail from a distance came by airplane.

When there were still four deliveries a day, the post office inaugurated same-day downtown service: mail picked up at postal collection boxes by 9 a.m. would be delivered that day. It was a heroic effort amid publicity over same-day service in London, but it drew little response and quietly died.

Letter carriers in those days were a disciplined lot. My carrier said that if he had a single letter left undelivered in his sorting case at the end of the day, he would find a written reprimand when he came to work the next morning.

Chapter Twenty
Scraps *on the* Cutting-Room Floor

Ripple Rock

    A fun story was the blowing up of Ripple Rock, the grave of many a ship on the inland passage to Alaska, a hundred miles north of Vancouver, B.C. I had an assignment in 1958 from both *Business Week* and *Popular Science* to tell ahead of time the what and the why of "man's greatest non-atomic underwater explosion." The reporting centered in Vancouver. Dot, our two girls and I turned this into a family outing that included an overnight at a delightful Provincial campground almost overlooking the whirlpools of Ripple Rock in Seymour Narrows.
    Ripple Rock was a seamount with twin domes, one only six feet from the surface at low tide, the other 20 feet down. The rock hid in the middle of a waterway that narrows from 20 miles to a half mile and makes a 90-degree turn. Tidal currents churned a white torrent around the rock. Eddies, whirlpools and cross-currents added to the treachery. An old pilot whom I sought out for an interview in Vancouver growled: "My piles stand on end every time I take a ship past Ripple Rock." Out of squeamishness of the time I softened the quote to say that his hair stood on end.
    The Canadian government tallied the toll the rock had taken as far back as 1875. In that year the Saranac, a U.S. warship of 11 guns, hit the rock and went down. Since then Ripple Rock sent to the bottom five large vessels and well over 100 fishing boats, tugs and yachts. The count of lives lost reached 114.

Many schemes were devised to blast the seamount, but none appeared practical until the Canadian government developed a plan to drill under the channel to the rock and blow it up from inside. With a $2.6-million contract, a crew of 60 hard-rock miners worked around the clock for two years. They began on Maud Island, an accessible base, and cut a mining shaft 7 by 18 feet straight down for 570 feet. There they turned the shaft to run level for 2,000 feet, then rise 300 feet into the twin domes. Smaller horizontal tunnels, 6 by 7 feet, fanned out near the top of the domes. These were packed with ammonium nitrate, a million and a half pounds sealed in 30,000 cans, 300 with fuses.

Explosives were placed deep enough in the rock to give ships clearance of at least 40 feet at low tide. There were no villages nearby that shock waves might damage, but a pulp mill five miles away at Elk Falls was shut down and evacuated on the day of detonation.

The explosion was set off from a shelter cut into bedrock on Quadra Island, one stepping stone beyond Maud Island. When the designated time came and the waterway was clear of all vessels, a nervous hand touched a match to a fuse that burned at an extraordinary speed. Motion-picture and still cameras with telescopic lenses, miles away, were ready. The news spread far across the continent and to those who never before heard of Seymour Narrows. The explosion was a spectacular success. Never again would Ripple Rock claw a ship's bottom. An extraordinary event, a fun story.

Seattle Magazine

The original *Seattle Magazine*, founded by Stimson Bullitt and published 1964-70, flirted with the newsletter, but the love was unrequited. Bullitt made two advances, both highly complimentary, but there was no match.

The magazine was one of the nation's early city magazines — sensitive, searching and well-written; edited by Peter Bunzel. But the going was rough. In retrospect, the magazine broke into print before Seattle had evolved enough in self-confidence and in breadth of leisure activities and social institutions to warrant an incisive monthly publication. [Bullitt's magazine had no connection with the *Seattle Magazine* of the 1990s.]

When the magazine was pushing hard to establish itself, Bullitt proposed binding the newsletter as an insert in the magazine. I didn't like the idea. What, for example, would happen to my subscribers outside the reach of the magazine? And if the magazine went bust, would I find myself holding an empty sack? Still, the proposal was flattering and at least worth exploring.

This was Bullitt's idea, and I should have asked him to come to my office to talk his idea through. But I was too aware how tawdry the Bay Building and my office might seem to a visitor accustomed to the glitter of a top law firm. People do not always recognize that what counts is not the setting but what comes out of it. I went to Bullitt's office. We talked, but the answer came down to no, thanks, Mr. Bullitt.

Some time afterward the magazine, losing money as it had from the outset, was preparing to close shop. When it quit, Stimson asked, may it offer Marple's Newsletter as one of three publications for subscribers to select for the unexpired portion of their subscription? The others were *New Republic* and *Pacific Search*, the latter published by Stimson's sister Harriet Bullitt.

Yes, indeed! I liked this for inexpensive sampling of a non-business audience. The magazine sent some 500 names from which, as best I can now piece out the records, the newsletter got 55 new subscribers. Every bit helped.

How Wide the Reach?

A question often asked: Where are most of your subscribers located? The pattern has held consistent from the outset: roughly two-thirds are in Seattle, the rim of Puget Sound, Portland, and the Willamette Valley. That of course is where most people of the Pacific Northwest live and do business. There also is a strong core of subscribers in Spokane and Boise, and a diverse scattering through the interior cities of farm and forest.

The newsletter also has a small but significant number of subscribers in California and the East who do business in the Pacific Northwest, and a sprinkling in Denmark, England and Japan.

Insider Transactions

I stumbled onto one slice of news that I found customers liked, Insider Transactions, a monthly report of purchases and sales by officers and directors of publicly held companies. At first I was reluctant to devote space to this list, but in the spread in ownership of Pacific Northwest stocks I found a growing interest. Investors check the list for clues as to how insiders regard their own company. I recall a subscriber's mentioning that, lunching with a friend, he pulled out of his pocket an issue of the newsletter with Insider Transactions and asked, "Did you see...?"

Insider Transactions remained a chore to prepare. The data came from a paperbound report of sometimes 200 pages issued monthly by the Securities and Exchange Commission. I'd take the report home and leaf through it in the evening to mark Pacific Northwest companies. Next day I'd type up the details to run in small type on page 4. Later the information became available by computer.

Investment Northwest

The growth and maturing of the economy brought an increase in the number of companies available to investors. As an eye-opening guide to the five big years 1967-1971, the newsletter ran a tabulation showing how the stock of each of 70 companies based in the Pacific Northwest or with significant operations here had grown — or shrunk — in market value. The report assumed purchase of $10,000 in stock at the start of 1967, added the shares gained from stock dividends and stock splits and calculated the value of the holdings after five years. This measured capital gains; it did not include cash dividends.

Most of the 70 companies beat the Dow Jones Industrial Average. The big gains came mainly in forest products, retailing and banking. Utilities changed little. Metals were in deep trouble. So was Boeing. Here is what an investment of $10,000 in 1967 became worth in five years:

In forest products: Pope & Talbot $53,100, Willamette Industries $32,960, Evans Products $26,460, and Weyerhaeuser $27,100. But Boise Cascade had shrunk to $8,510. In other lines: Fred Meyer $35,420, Safeco $22,080, Paccar $21,780, Marine Bancorp (later Rainier) $18,040, Seafirst Bank $16,700.

But there were also some big losers: Kaiser Aluminum $4,790, Anaconda $3,830, and Oregon Metallurgical $2,190. Boeing, in the midst of severe cutback, had shrunk to $2,730.

Odd Jobs

The gathering of news brought sometimes an unusual assignment from New York. One of my steady customers was the daily *Bond Buyer*, the bible on municipal bonds — those issued by states, counties, cities, water districts, public utility districts and other units of government. Electric utilities were especially in the news in the development with Bonneville Power Administration of an integrated network, from British Columbia to California. Dams built with U.S. dollars on the upper Columbia River in Canada steadied the flow of snowmelt from the Canadian Rockies and thus squeezed more dollars from water flowing past dams in the U.S.

When the British Columbia Parliament voted to take over the largest electric utility in the province, the *Bond Buyer* asked for a detailed account of the what, the why, and as much as possible of the consequences. Out of this came a lead article in a special number of the *Bond Buyer* issued for the annual convention of the Investment Bankers Association of America, meeting that year in Vancouver, B.C.

The conservative *Bond Buyer* played this under bold type: "Canadian Bombshell: British Columbia Expropriates $727 Million Electric Utility - by Elliot Marple." The expropriation, the article set out, was "certain to affect the electric power industry not only of western Canada but of the western United States as well. It also touched money markets half-way around the world."

Another Customer for News

A customer of quite another sort was the quarterly four-page letter of Pacific First Federal Savings & Loan Association, Tacoma. With offices from Bellingham to Eugene, Pacific First was much the largest S&L in the Pacific Northwest. It published *Business and Real Estate Trends* as a goodwill builder. The first three pages, spruced up with charts, contained national news written in the East. But the back page provided a back-home touch under the heading, "A Look at the Pacific Northwest." This page carried the signature of Gerrit Vander Ende, president.

It was my job for some 20 years to write the back page, a project headed by Ernest A. Messenger. Earlier, like numerous newcomers, Messenger found his way to my office looking for suggestions on a company worth tying up with. He had come out of the financial world in Chicago and soon became a resourceful vice-president under Vander Ende.

The back page was Messenger's idea and responsibility. He and I would work out the subject for the next issue, then I'd dig in. An early back page headed "Wooden Dollars" talked of the place of lumber and plywood as payroll builders. Another, "Show Case of the Orient," centered on an international trade fair in Seattle. "The Boat Boom" focused on pleasure boating and the Pacific Northwest as a leader in U.S. boat-building. "Winter Fun on High Slopes" took the reader to the snow country. Of course there was also one on "Boeing, Cornerstone of the Economy." An early report on "Electronics in the Northwest" cited three key factors in the look ahead and concluded with what must be the understatement of the decade, "The years ahead are certain to bring further growth."

It was fun to prepare the back page, written for a broader audience than business. The issues of *Trends*, three months apart, gave plenty of time to develop a topic of interest to the thousands who had a savings account or a mortgage with Pacific First. Some of the material and perspective spilled over from reporting for my newsletter, but every issue sent me out talking to a dozen or so specialists, and brisk condensation carried readers to a fresh glimpse of the land where they lived and worked.

There is a sequel. Ernie Messenger remained with Pacific First until his retirement. He was loyal, devoted, and a ceaseless worker. One day well after retirement, I found him almost bitter about the lame reward for a long, productive career. Retirement of course brought a company pension, but that was all. Pacific First was a mutual company; it had no stockholders. Had Ernie worked for a bank or manufacturer whose stock was publicly traded, he could have bought the company's stock as an investment and likely also have received stock options. As many in industry have found, options can sweeten a pension several-fold.

Messenger is dead. His complaint was valid. Stock options are incentive and reward in any growing company and sometimes add millions to the compensation of key people — as some of the top officers at Washington Mutual found after that thrift built itself into the largest savings institution in the country.

Nordstrom

Nordstrom, the specialty store that operates in carefully selected cities across the country, made the transition from family ownership to public ownership more than 20 years ago. The company was known for a time as Nordstrom-Best, an interim name after Nordstrom, famed for its shoe stores, acquired Best's Apparel for expansion into women's wear.

Money for new stores came from earnings and also from the company's initial sale of public stock. The transition to public ownership is a fidgety time for any company. Financial details once closely guarded have to be thrown open. There would be reporters to talk to, some perhaps new to the business world and groping along. In doing an early profile of the company I asked for an interview on the basis that "you're better off to have a fair and balanced story by someone accustomed to working with business."

The interview and the story went together well. Some time afterward Everett Nordstrom, one of the three brothers who built Nordstrom nationwide, wrote: "May I thank you for writing such an accurate, factual report? One of the reasons for being reluctant to provide such information to the press has been our previous disappointments in inaccuracies which have resulted. We were, therefore, very pleased to find that you had written a story that was so acceptable and complimentary to us."

Over the years investors in Nordstrom have done well. The initial public offering in 1971 priced Nordstrom stock at $24.50 a share. An investment of $2,450 shares for 100 shares in that offering would have grown through stock splits and stock dividends to 4,800 shares having at a peak in mid-1998 a market value of $192,000. In addition to this capital gain the stock has paid a small dividend in cash every year.

Another Retailer

The Pacific Northwest has produced a number of leaders in their field — innovators who in time earned national attention. One of several spotted in the newsletter was David J. Heerensperger, who in 1970 at age 33 moved to the top of Pay 'N Pak, a four-state chain geared to do-it-yourselfers. Heerensperger founded his first store with $300 in capital, pushed how-to-do-it instruction in building materials, and later merged with similar stores founded by Stan Thurman and John M. Headley.

The newsletter's initial profile of the company picked up "last week's simple announcement of a change in top officers," told of a "bitter split" among the three founders, and carried financial details including wide divergence in top salaries. "We had a lot of rivalry to overcome," Heerensperger acknowledged. After the newsletter's account came out Heerensperger grumped enough about the candor of my reporting to leave me uneasy — until he mentioned that his wife thought the account was fair.

The chain grew. Stockholders made money. Then the company was bought out. Heerensperger left. But the new management lost the consumer touch. The company went into bankruptcy and disappeared. That left a clearer field to Ernst Hardware, a decades-old multi-state chain much larger then than Pay 'N Pak. I recalled Heerensperger's offhand comment when I first visited Pay 'N Pak headquarters: "What an opportunity if one could only take over Ernst Hardware."

Years passed. Ernst faltered, lost money, sold stock in a desperate move to raise capital. In 1996 it, too, disappeared in bankruptcy. One factor widely credited for Ernst's collapse was the competition of a brash new company, Eagle Hardware and Garden, organized in the 1990s on the original Pay 'N Pak formula of guidance for the do-it-yourselfer. Now Eagle offered much more: mammoth stores, an incredible range of inventory, and buying power with its suppliers that enabled it to emphasize rock-bottom prices at retail. Eagle was riding the wave of mega-stores.

And who was the founder and builder of Eagle? David J. Heerensperger. He continued as chairman until 1997. Late that year a filing with the Securities and Exchange Commission disclosed the market value of his holdings of Eagle stock exceeded $62 million.

Observations Along the Way

Anyone who publishes a newsletter is often asked how to start a new one. It looks so easy. When a friend on the *Vancouver Sun* asked about launching a business letter for western Canada, I wrote that "in a sense a four-page newsletter is a mood piece; it presents information but it does so in a way that carries a mood, or an impression, broader or stronger than the bare information. Facts alone don't do the job." But I cautioned that he seemed too concerned about format and frequency, details that come later. He needed first to analyze his market. When he did, he dropped the project.

About this time I put together for another inquiry "notes on writing for a newsletter." Some points:

"A general-interest newsletter is tough to write. Done well, it reads with clarity and directness and retains some of the drama of the events we're talking about. It requires writing and rewriting, frequently a half-dozen times through the typewriter....

"Background is extremely important — background, perspective and insight. That is where we differ from a daily paper....

"Don't try to tell it all in the first sentence or the first paragraph; the reader can't grasp significant ideas that fast. Let the story unfold in sequence, the way it happened; don't kill the natural drama as newspapers do by starting with the conclusion and then backing up to fill in the details....

"The writing has to be fresh, lively, distinctive. The language is that of conversation. When you find yourself using a cliché, ask yourself: 'What am I really trying to say.' Then say it.

"Use strong verbs. You want action. Avoid the easy trap of the various forms of *to be*, the weakest verb in the English language ....Make every word earn its way....

"Write with conviction. That means you have to know what you are talking about. There is nothing harder than to discover as you start to write that you are not sure of your material and don't have the detail or grasp....

"Write it, then let it sit. When you come back to the story you are apt to say: 'How could I have done anything so crummy, so dull?' Many a story that looked finished and in final form at the end of Saturday was totally rewritten on Monday just before the deadline."

A random note to a publicity man trying to plant a story: "You are crossing from the advertising side to the editorial side. You are not getting paid advertising. What you are getting is the currency of an idea. The space or time you can command depends on the strength or vitality of your idea."

A note to myself: "Do not fall in love with words — words for their own sake. Fall in love with ideas. Words are only a tool to convey ideas. Don't be carried away by the tool."

Chapter Twenty-One
The Maturing of a Region

By the late 1980s the Pacific Northwest economy had reached a significant turn, a change in direction recognized only slowly. Five rough backwoods states — Washington, Oregon, Idaho, Montana and Alaska — had limped out of World War II not sure what might turn up but stretching, reaching, hoping. Their economies remained tied to the richness of nature — forests, farms, fish, mines and seaports.

"Looking back," I wrote Miner Baker shortly before his death in 1997, "the newsletter got its start in a brief niche of time that long since closed."

That niche extended from the end of World War II to the start of the computer or high-tech age. In that time a generation of leaders built a new Pacific Northwest. They put up mills to create products and jobs from the forest. They added plants to convert nature's reward of fruits and vegetables into products ready for the kitchen. They drew electric power from the Columbia and Snake rivers (now so controversial) to bring in the light-metals and chemical industries. They brought irrigation water to rich but parched desert land. They built an aircraft industry known the world over. They diversified in manufacturing and services to supply markets at home and overseas. Is there another segment of the United States where four decades brought such change?

Out of this period, this effort, came national recognition for the region and, more important, a self-confidence, a love for the region as a place to spend one's life, and a belief that great things can be done as well here as in any other part of the country.

The maturing of this corner of the country has been hastened and strengthened by the emergence of the computer industry. Indeed, it is hard to overstate the importance of the computer, the greatest new industrial tool since the internal combustion engine a century ago, ranking perhaps with the harnessing of electriciy. Ahead lie changes as unpredictable and yet as far-reaching as those that followed the automobile. The Pacific Northwest enters this era with world recognition.

The computer or high tech industry adds a fresh layer to the region's economy, a new dimension, not in place of but on top of the well-established resource-based economy. It builds not on oil or steel or timber but on brain power. It draws investment capital from around the country on a scale this region has never seen. It knows no limitation of geography; the cost of freight to world markets forms no barrier. The development and production of computer software and hardware has displaced the century-old forest industry as the region's No. l pocketbook filler.

Of Microsoft, has there ever been a company, or an industry, that prized so highly and paid so well for people with the ability to think and to tackle opportunity only dimly perceived? New software takes brains first, and then capital. Innovation requires not elaborate and costly machinery (as in a new textile mill, a paper mill, or auto assembly line) but an extraordinary banking of intelligence — and with this an attitude of the joy of search, of daring, and delight in building anew. No one can see where this may lead in the century just ahead.

Look back for perspective. Two quirks of geography shaped the Pacific Northwest economy. Call them, if you prefer, happenstance, events that could have occurred anywhere but fortunately happened here. Their impact reaches around the world.

The first was the happenstance that a man named Bill Boeing grew up in Seattle and took to flying when airplanes were a toy. Out of his ventures came the company that carries his name and grew in World War II into a military powerhouse. Postwar, as Boeing struggled for commercial markets, the accident of the death of its president Philip Johnson brought William Allen to the top. With him, and following him, came daring leadership that made Boeing the largest manufacturer north of San Francisco and first in the world in commercial aircraft.

The second was the happenstance that Bill Gates and Paul Allen were born in Seattle. They teamed up to found Microsoft. The company built world dominance in its field and cash reserves stretching incredibly into the billions of dollars. Microsoft's base was not the old stalwarts of timber, metals and oil, but brain power. It draws to its headquarters on the edge of Seattle scientists, engineers, researchers and managers from across the country and overseas — a leavening of unmeasured consequence that extends all through the civic and social community.

Without those two quirks of geography the Pacific Northwest would remain a region of vastly less consequence today.

CHAPTER TWENTY-TWO
Mike Parks Takes Over

Some years ago Don Redfern, a director of Greenacres, Inc., a small publicly held company in forestry, kept pushing its president, Mike Lazara: "Mike, if you are working on today's problems, you are not doing the job you were hired for. You've got to look way ahead." Redfern was relentless. At another time he insisted: "Your job is to train your successor." Lazara, buried in operating detail, groaned. But Redfern, then head of an expanding chemical manufacturer in Seattle but not now living, spoke doctrine. What he said applied just as much to me at the newsletter.

Bruce McKim photo - 1976
Mike Parks

Continuity is so hard to build in a small business. In early days of the newsletter I had hoped to bring in a reporter and build from there. Years went by, the newsletter grew, I passed the conventional retirement age and still had no one to take over. What I was looking for was simple: a person who had some understanding of business, who could write clearly, and was a self-starter. I think "self-starter" was the greatest requirement. The newsletter had no room for a person whose talent lay in coming to work promptly each morning, all smiles, shoes shined, and asking: "What do I do today?" There had to be a curiosity that sharpened perception and sent one looking and digging.

There was also, of course, an element of luck in finding a match. Over the years I talked to several persons at length but always came away discouraged. A reporter in Portland followed up our talk by sending a sample to show that, yes, he really knew how to write a newsletter. Oh, my! I wish I had saved his try. It dripped with a beginner's concept of style rather than substance; hackneyed, incredibly loaded with clichés including that oh-so-tired, "Look for...."

Another and more likely prospect was a public relations man in San Francisco whose company had ties to the Pacific Northwest. We swapped notes, then he and his wife came up for a look-see. In the final evening with dinner at my house we had delightful conversation, so much so that the visitors missed their flight home. But later we came separately to the same conclusion: No. Although he worried about the security of his job in a big company, he shied away from a small company where so much would depend on what he himself did. For my part I did not see in him the relentless drive of a self-starter.

George Cheek and I talked a bit, but never seriously. I regarded him highly from his work in public relations at the American Plywood Association in Tacoma. He could easily have taken over the newsletter. He came from Spokane and later returned there to set up his own shop.

I don't recall the first time I met Mike Parks, but I ran into him occasionally in reporting on business. He came to a press conference well prepared, as most reporters did not, and he often had a leading question to ask after others had left.

From his first job on the *Spokesman-Review* in Spokane Mike moved to the news staff of the *Seattle Times* and in time became financial editor. I read his daily stuff carefully. He understood business. His analysis was much the best of anyone around. He was then in his

162 Elliot Marple

Marple's Business Newsletter
Covering the Pacific Northwest since 1949

COLMAN BUILDING, SEATTLE 98104   206/622-0155

*Hi Elliot and Mike —
All of us @ P6C sure agree w/ this statement!
You fellows do a superb job.
Sincerely,
Bob Peters*

October 18, 1978

A report to readers:

The other day the mail brought us the very pleasant and unexpected bouquet in the quarterly economic bulletin of Pacific First Federal Savings & Loan Association. After commending the "competent, objective and constructive" business reporting in newspapers of Washington and Oregon, H. Dewayne Kreager, president and chairman, wrote:

> To top it all off there is the nation's outstanding regional business newsletter, written and published every two weeks for 30 years by Elliot Marple of Seattle, and now with his new associate, Michael J. Parks. If there is a regional publication anywhere that can equal Marple's Business Newsletter, I have never seen it. Few people truly appreciate what a great asset Marple's has been to business and government in these two states.

Thanks, Mr. Kreager! We appreciate that all the more because it comes from an economist of national reputation who made Pacific First Federal into the first billion-dollar savings and loan association north of San Francisco.

The number of our readers continues to grow, as it has in each year since our start at a time when there was mighty little business reporting anywhere in the Pacific Northwest.

Today's issue goes to 3,600 subscribers. Most of them -- over 90%, in fact -- work right here in the Pacific Northwest. But we have also had a surprising jump (41%) in the past year in the number of subscribers in the Midwest and East -- St. Louis, Chicago, Cleveland, Charlotte, New York, Stamford, Boston, for example. The interest in those areas, of course, reflects the growing national recognition of the expanding economy in this far corner of the country.

Readers often ask: Where do you get your news? Certainly not sitting at a desk or reading other publications. Primarily we get the news by going out and talking to men and women who are making news. Sometimes we start with the briefest of items and build up the perspective that gives significance to the news and makes it important to a wider segment of business. In this we start with our own background knowledge and files, and then go out for interviews. We check first the company that's making the news, but we also cross-check with bankers, suppliers, customers or competitors to get balance.

Good ideas for newsletter items sometimes come in from you subscribers, who after all represent every segment of the economy and just about every type of business in the Pacific Northwest. Please give us a call or drop us a note any time you spot something we ought to work on or a topic on which you would like information. We'll do our best.

Sincerely,

Elliot Marple   Michael J. Parks

Kreager: "The nation's outstanding business newsletter"

middle 30s, a generation younger than I. From time to time we chatted about the newsletter.

Then one day he came at my invitation to talk seriously. It would be a long leap for Mike. At the *Times* he was in the midst of the hum and bustle of a couple of hundred reporters and editors. He wrote a daily story "by Michael J. Parks." He had recognition in the business community and the security of a retirement system. And just a sidelight, he was gambler enough to join fellow newsmen for an occasional evening of low-stakes poker.

Benham Studio, 1999

Michael J. Parks

By contrast, *Marple's Business Newsletter* could only seem somber. Its workshop was just a long, quiet room. Its staff consisted only of Marple and Mrs. Bertram, the latter still only part-time. There was no 40-hour week, no union contract guaranteeing minimum pay, no medical benefits, no pension, and no retirement plan. Mike's decision was not easy. Ahead loomed the expense of college for three youngsters. But he recognized the reputation and by now the respectable earnings of the newsletter and he had ideas for building the letter and its following.

In January 1977 Mike came to work at the newsletter, a reporter on salary with the understanding that if it was a fit he could gradually buy the company with his share of earnings. He voluntarily resigned as the Seattle stringer for *The Wall Street Journal* to avoid conflict with *Business Week*, which I still handled and for which Mike would also write.

Three years later Mike took over as the newsletter's editor and publisher and soon after became sole owner. He was free to change the name but chose not to. I continue as a corporate director, and Mike and I remain close friends.

Mike Parks grew up in the age of the computer, of high technology. He came to the newsletter in the transition of the economy from a resource base to the emerging world of the computer. He keeps tabs on the old while searching out the new. Just as I wrote of wood products as the basic industry of an earlier day, Mike writes of high technology and spotlights emerging companies, one after another.

Mike has also made the computer a tool in the production of the newsletter. The day has passed, fortunately, when the subscription list of 4,000 was kept on 3x5 file cards and metal addressplates, and in the heads of Marple and Mrs. Bertram.

Miner Baker, who in retirement wrote a column for the *Seattle Post-Intelligencer*, once singled out the newsletter as the prime source for business news and added a warm word of Mike Parks as editor and publisher. Miner wrote:

"Marple's is a classic in regional business letters. Founded in 1949 by Elliot Marple, it quickly established a reputation for thoroughness and accuracy. Elliot was a unique blend of reporter and economic analyst with an indefatigable thirst for the story behind the story. He dug out facts like an investigative reporter but he never used them to embarrass....

"Marple...built on quality. As a regional economist myself, I used to wonder where Elliot got all his stuff. The answer was generally that he was out working at it and eternally asking questions.

"Equally as remarkable...as the reputation Elliot built was the fact that he passed it on untarnished to a man with the same dogged determination and intellectual curiosity. Mike Parks joined Elliot in 1977. Elliot retired from the newsletter in 1981. There was never a hitch in the continuity."

Sometimes I am asked: "Would you do it again, start a newsletter from nothing and go through the hard early years with 'blood on the typewriter keys'?"

Yes, certainly yes!

To dare, to push ahead however rough the way, to know that, though the project may not be great, your destiny lies in your own hands. That is the exhilaration of life. It is cut from the American dream.

Benham Studio, 1999

Two publishers, 50 years
Michael J. Parks and Elliot Marple

APPENDIX
Subscribers Talk Back

Letters in the formative years suggest by the names of writers the range of appeal and by comment give clues as to what readers look for in a regional business letter. For example:

"You did a splendid job on the power contract situation. Your summary is very well balanced and should be helpful in developing public understanding....I hope you will drop in to see us any time you have the opportunity."
—John Dierdorff, v.p., Pacific Power & Light, Portland, August 7, 1951.

"I know that you realize that we are a part of the Pacific Northwest because your map on the letterhead points that out very clearly, but I am sensitive about the matter as much as practically every government agency has tied us in with the Twin Cities."
—Robert A. McCann, Missoula Chamber of Commerce, August 14, 1951.

"You are to be complimented on your concise, accurate write up of the Pacific Northwest Steel Warehouse situation.
—W. J. Ulrich, Pacific Machinery & Tool Steel Co., Portland, October 24, 1951.

"Very good paper. Believe better than Kiplinger because of specifics."
—H. J. Chandler, Radio KFLW, Klamath Falls, October 13, 1952.

"Would it be possible for me to order 200 copies of the Wednesday, July 2d edition?" [steel strike]
—Fred Goddard, KXRO, Aberdeen, July 23, 1952.

"We are interested in expanding our sawmill machinery business and the Roundup is a good source of information on which we base some plans."
—William K. Stamets, Jr., Enterprise Co., Columbiana, Ohio, December 6, 1952.

"The next time you are in Portland I will show you some membership rosters which will give the names and addresses of business men who are, or should be, interested in the Roundup."
—Sid Woodbury, Woodbury Co., Portland, December 18, 1952.

"Last week I was in need of a quick appraisal of the tourist industry in the Northwest when your letter arrived providing a nicely condensed summary."
—L. F. Growney, Pacific Power and Light Co., Portland, June 30, 1953.

"Could you advise me if there is a newsletter similar to yours printed in the San Francisco area? I am being transferred to the Bay Area."
—Ralph V. Walthers, Gillette Safety Razor Co., Portland, September 7, 1955.

"I envy you the ability to grasp a subject in some other field and express it so accurately....I should appreciate the courtesy of letting me have a few extra copies. I shall want to mail them to some of the key men I expect to see in the next few days in Washington."
—Ben H. Hazen, president, Benj. Franklin Federal Saving and Loan Assn., Portland, January 17, 1956.

"We are very much interested in your article regarding Growth of Pacific Northwest Credit Unions in Newsletter No. 206. Please tell us where we might write to get further information."
—Milton A. Hickey; Cornell, Howland, Hayes & Merryfield, Corvallis, May 14, 1957.

"Our interest in the Roundup is based less on your coverage of the lumber industry (although I was very interested in your December 11 report on changes contemplated by some Plywood manufacturers) than on the general economic information which you provide."
—William Dean, Lumbermen's Buying Service, Eugene, December 19, 1957.

"Have eliminated several 'dope' sheets in favor of yours."
—Franz Ridgway, Courtesy Credit Corp., Portland, August 13, 1958.

"Your May 13 double-header has a lot of good solid dope that I am glad to have in my own planning."
—Lewis B. Reynolds, Walker's Manual, San Francisco, May 18, 1959.

"Thank you for mentioning our Chemical Industry study ....Through today's mail we have received 67 letters and telephone calls requesting 107 copies of the report, all of them mentioning they read about the study in your newsletter."
—Stewart G. Neel, Puget Sound Power & Light, Seattle, July 21, 1960.

"Many thanks for the very nice mention of Redco. I am amazed at your coverage, having received calls from all over the Northwest and from every type of business."
—M. E. Hillman, Republic Electric & Development Co., Seattle, April 25, 1961.

"It was a pleasure to read your [newsletter] of November 8. I had talked quite freely and frankly to you about our company and our industry, and afterward I wondered what you were going to do with the material. I suppose every businessman feels a little nervous and uncomfortable talking to someone who is going to use some - but not all - of the material that he gathers as a result of a conversation of this kind....

"I want to congratulate you on having distilled out of our conversation, and the conversation you had with others in our industry, the essential facts. You not only kept your facts straight, but you also managed to get the proper emphasis."
—Ken Fisher, Fisher Flouring Mills Co., Seattle, November 10, 1961.

"My personal thanks for your very constructive article ...regarding the Center for Graduate Studies and the Industrial Research Institute in Portland."
—Douglas C. Strain, president, Electro Scientific Industries, Portland, January 23, 1963.

"This is a long overdue fan letter. Your lucid discussion of automation and its widening applications...rocked me off dead center....Over the years you've conditioned me to expect nothing less than precision, accuracy, lucidity, and thoroughness in the Roundup as well as your reports to Business Week, but I tend to forget that unlike the rest of us who have a whole forest of editors to keep us on track, your discipline is entirely self-imposed."
—Richard Lamb, West Coast editor, Business Week, San Francisco, June 5, 1963.

"As an avid and regular reader...I compliment you on the clear, concise coverage you furnish on business, industry and economics of the Pacific Northwest...the best single source of information on this important market."
—Irvine B. Rabel, Star Machinery, Seattle, June 20, 1963.

"With tight credit policies like this, you ought to be rich before now."
—Alan Bradley, president, Capital Investors Corp., Missoula, after receiving a "Sorry, last copy" and then renewing, February 26, 1964.

"The writeup was factual, interesting and accurate."
—Gordon Tongue, Ideal Cement Co., Seattle, December 17, 1964.

"Sometimes it is so accurate it scares me."
—Ron Richardson, Crown Zellerbach, Seattle, January 6, 1966.

"It always amazes me how you can take a basketful of disjointed information and put it together in a smoothly flowing narrative with just enough statistics to tell the story."
—Kenneth S. Hodge, Clark County Industrial Bureau, Vancouver, Washington, February 1, 1968.

"....that wonderful letter. Many people attempt to write letters and some of them are pretty good. Some of them are only a repetition of what somebody else has already said and, as a result, are time-wasters. Your letter is always worth reading, and the language is good, the facts have been researched and it is a real pleasure to read the news of the Northwest through such a wonderful medium."
—W. H. Hunt, exec. v.p., George-Pacific, Portland, October 23, 1969.

"If all reporters were as precise as you are, giving interviews would be a pleasure."
—R. P. Wollenberg, president, Longview Fibre, Longview, September 5, 1970.

"You're not trying to hurt some one the way a lot of newspaper guys do. You are not trying to cut someone up to make things more interesting. You are not going in for a bunch of hogwash."
—Gus Asplund, v.p., Seattle-First National Bank, December 22, 1971.

When, doing a story for *Business Week* on pulp & paper, I needed some reporting from industry leaders outside the Pacific NW. Richard Lamb assigned Duane Anderson of his San Francisco staff to interview Reid Hunt, president and CEO, Crown Zellerbach. Anderson's subsequent note to me: "When I told Hunt this was for you, he chuckled and said: 'I wonder what I can say about the industry that Marple doesn't already know.'"

July 6, 1974.

"There is less integrity in the free enterprise system than I have ever known. You've got integrity in your news sheet and you can get information that others can't. Just keep it that way."
—*Edward Phelan, manager, Seattle Retail Trade Bureau, November 21, 1974.*

"Naturally we do not always find it pleasant to read about our errors. Nevertheless, we felt the report [on Evans Products] was fair and factual."
—*Gerald A. Parsons, v.p., Evans Products Co., Portland, May 7, 1975.*

"Your May 7 story on Evans Products was a prize-winning effort in business reporting — obviously well researched, documented, humanized with the personalities involved and loaded with interesting detail."
—*B. K. Forman, Burlington Northern, Seattle, May 9, 1975.*

"It is amazing to me how you could in a page and a half cover so many important points in the almost 30-year history of our company and make it so understandable with such continuity."
—*H. J. Musiel, Westours, December 17, 1975.*

"Have you ever considered raising your price? On the basis of the caliber of the letter and its worth you can charge substantially more. We'd pay three or four times as much."
—Hal Meden, v.p., Esterline Corp., Bellevue, October 22, 1976.

Your newsletter "is probably the most accurate business report of events in the state to be found outside of Alaska."
—William J. Bell, economist, National Bank of Alaska, Anchorage, November 5, 1976.

Of the year-end issue, "it continues to amaze me how you crank out such quality work with a small staff."
— John MacKenzie, Foster & Marshall, Seattle, January 6, 1977.

INDEX

Abbott, Leith E., 46
Ace Tank & Equipment, 60
Acheson, Robert, 77
Advertising Age, 17, 28-29
Agricultural Extension Service, 98, 107.
Allen, Paul, 159
Allen, William, 159
American-Marietta, 115
American Smelting & Refining, 115
Anaconda Copper, 115, 116, 150
APA-The Engineered Wood Assn, 125
Asplund, Gus, 169
Assn of Washington Industries, 41
Atomic Energy Commission, 116

Baker, Miner H., 58, 164
Bank earnings and outlook, 88-93
Bank of America, 134, 136
Bay Building, 111-114
Beaupre, Robert 26.
Bell, William J., 170
Bernstein, Sid, 28.
Bertram, Helen, 113-114, 126, 133
Black Ball Freight Line, 77
Blake, Moffitt & Towne, 47
Bloomberg, Ray, 109
Boeing, 21, 26, 116, 127, 150, 159

Boeing, William, 158
Boise Cascade, 21, 64, 70-72, 115, 120, 150
Bond Buyer, 151
Bonneville Power Administration, 150
Borden, 115
Bowles, Chester, 9
Bradley, Alan, 168
British Columbia power, 150
Brown, Ralph, 72-74
Building permits, 91
Bullitt, Harriet, 148
Bullitt, Stimson, 147-148
Bunker Hill Co., 115, 122-123
Bunzel, Peter, 148
Burke Building, 13, 110
Burwell, George, 60
Business Week, 9, 12, 19, 24, 25, 28, 61-67

Campbell, W.L. (Wigs), 61
Carlson, Maxwell, 129-137
Chandler, H.J., 165.
Cheek, George, 161
Clark, Walter, 11, 23
Cohen, Stan, 17
Colborn, Robert, 64
Computer industry, 95 ff.
Conner, Guy W., 47
Conroy, Jim, 110
Credit Bureau, Snohomish, 57
Crown Zellerbach, 116, 169

Dean, William, 167
Dickinson, Phillips, 47

Dierdorff, John, 165
Doane Agricultural Services, 98, 107
Documentary Book Publishers, 141
Douglas Fir Plywood Assn, 124

Eagle Hardware & Garden, 154
East's Bindery, 111
Employment leaders, 116, 127, plywood, 124
Engle, A.B., 45
Ernst Hardware, 154
Evans Products, 150

Fairchild Publications, 10
Faragher, Robert, 133
Farwell, Hollis, 47
Federal Land Bank, Spokane, 108
Federal Reserve, San Francisco, 58, 93
First National Bank, Portland, 88, 90
Fisher, Ken, 168
Food Field Reporter, 17, 28, 69
Food Topics, 30-31
Foote, Cone & Belding, 46
Ford Motor, 57
Forest industry, in change, 70-75
Forman, B.K., 170
Frankland, Charles, 30
Fred Meyer, 68, 150
Frederick & Nelson, 56
Freightliner, 141

Garden of Allah, 111, 114
Gates, Bill, 159
Gemeroy, Gordon, 29

General Petroleum, 115
Georgia-Pacific, 64, 115, 124
Giannini, A.P., 79
Gilbert, Elon J., 105, 107
Gleed, Thomas F., 139
Goddard, Fred, 165
Granducci, Oeveste, 42-44
Great Northern, 14, 116
Greenacres, Inc., 160
Growney, L.F., 166
Grunwald, Ed, 19, 26, 64-66

Hahn, Ruth, 24
Hall, L.V., 47
Hansberger, Robert V., 70-71
Hanna, 115
Harry & David, 32
Harvey Aluminum, 115
Hazen, Ben H., 166
Headley, John M., 154
Heerensperger, David J., 154
Herwig, Ed-E, 11
Hickey, Milton A., 166
Hillman, M.E., 167
Hobson, Karl, 82, 98-108
Hodge, Kenneth S., 169
House, Tom, 81
Huber, Louis, 109
Hunt, Reid, 169
Hunt, W.H., 169
Hutton, E.F., & Co., 47

Industry profile, 115-117; 126-128

Inland Empire Industrial Research, 46
Inn at Harbor Steps, 114
Insider transactions, 149
Insurance industry, 94
Investments Northwest, 136, 140, 149, 153, 154

Jackson, Phil, 34
Jenkins, Florence, 109
John Fluke Mfg Co, 96
Johnson, Philip, 159
Jondal, Herm, 51, 111

Kaiser Aluminum, 150
Kotkins, Henry L., 22.
Kiplinger Washington Letter, 42, 44, 57, 62
Kreager, H. Dewayne, 162
Kritikos, Nicholas T., 131

LA-Seattle Motor Express, 83
Labor unions in forest industry, 72; in mining, 122
Lamb, Richard, 10, 12, 19-21, 24, 33, 38, 46,
  63-64, 168
Lazara, Michael, 160
Lewis, C.W., 125
Lewis, Douglas B., 47
Linfield Research Institute, 96
Louisiana Forestry Assn, 125
Lyman, Frank, 80, 112

MacKenzie, G.B., 57
MacKenzie, John, 170
Marine Bancorp, 88, 150; (see Natl Bank of Commerce)
Marple, Barbara, 86, 131

Marple, Dorotha, 7, 16, 34, 45, 48, 86, 126, 131
Marple, Elliot, arrival in Seattle, 8; Washington, D.C., 9, 16; first office, 13, 14; a look back 15 years, 15; news bureau, 16; work schedule and pay, 30; newsletter takes form, 34; the help of Miner Baker, 58; the help of Sam McFadden, 76; farm letter, 98; office help, 110; investment policy, 120; a month off, 126-128; retired, 164
Marple, Lucius E. (father), 32, 38, 51
Marple, Warren (brother), 12, 53
Marple's Business Newsletter, new name, 38; number of subscribers, 55, 128, 148; 10-year issue, 115; promotion, 117; writing a newsletter, 155
Marple's Business Roundup, founding, 36 ff.; promotion, 47-ff.; style, 49-52
Maxon Inc., Detroit, 8-9, 22
McCann, Robert A., 165
McCarty, Richard, 47-48, 110
McFadden, Eleanor, 79, 86
McFadden, S.D., 10, 11, 24, 27, 41, 52, 69, 76-87
McGraw-Hill, 10, 33
Meden, Hal, 170
Messenger, Ernest A., 151
Micron Technology, 95
Microsoft, 64, 93, 158
Miller, Roy, 10
Milwaukee RR, 116
Mine, Mill & Smelter Union, 122-123
Modern Packaging, 24, 35
Monsanto, 115
Morgan, Howard W., 46
Musiel, H.J., 170

Natl Assn of Manufacturers, 21
Natl Bank of Commerce, 59, 119, 129-137
Neel, Stewart G., 167
New England Fish Co., 69, 83

New York Times, 51
Niendorff, Fred, 34
Nike, 19, 64
Nordstrom retailer, 64, 153
Nordstrom, Everett, 153
Northern Pacific, 14, 116, 130, 142
Northwest Canners Assn, 28
Northwest Cold Pack, 78
Northwest Metal Products, 143

O'Connor, Lucille, Jack, 8, 17
Office of Price Administration, 9, 20
Olson, Bruce H., 130-131
Oregonian, 34
Oregon Journal, 34, 109
Oregon Metallurgical, 150
Orton, George, 104

Paccar, 21, 33, 64, 119, 138-141, 143, 150
Pacific First S&L, 90, 151
Pacific National Bank, 29. 88
PacifiCorp, 95
Pacific Telephone, 116
Pacific Waxed Paper, 45
Parker, Oren, 72
Pay'N Pak, 154
Parks, Michael, 48, 59, 67, 114, 117, 120, 135, 160-164
Parsons, Gerald A., 170
Parsons, W.B., 45
Perspective on Pacific NW, 115, 125, 157, 159
Phelan, Edward, 170
Phillips-Pacific, 115
Pigott, Charles, 140

Pigott, Mark, 141
Pigott, Paul, 33, 139
Plywood industry moves South, 123-125
Pollock, David, 117
Pope & Talbot, 150
Popular Science, 146
Postal service, 144
Potlatch Forests, 115
Power, electric, 49, 150
Price, Andrew, 129, 131
Price, Andrew Jr., 130-131, 133
Produce News, 69
Provorse, Barry, 141
Public relations, 9, 11, 156
Puget Sound Naval Shipyard, 116

QFC stores, 68

Rabel, Irvine B., 168
Rainier National Bank, 136
Railroads, 142-145
Redfern, Don, 160
Reeves, Mr. & Mrs. Carl, 8
Reichhold, 115
Restaurant Management, 11, 23
Reynolds, Bryce, 118
Reynolds, Lewis B., 119, 167
Richardson, Ron, 169
Ridgway, Franz, 167
Rippey, Steve, 10
Ripple Rock, B.C., 146
Ross, Dudley, 35
Ryan, Howard, 46.

Safeco, 95, 150
Sales Management, 24, 31
Salmon Bay Sand & Gravel, 58
Savings & loan assns, 90-93
Sawyers, Helen B., 57
Schaal, Norbert, 13, 49, 113
Schwab, C. E., 123
Schwartz, Harry S., 58
Scott Paper, 115
Seattle Bronze, 47
Seattle-First Natl Bank, 58, 128, 129, 136, 150
Seattle, housing, 17
Seattle Magazine, 147-148
Seattle Post-Intelligencer, 34
Seattle Times, 32, 34, 161
Security Pacific Bank, 135
Shanahan, Eileen, 51
Shell Refinery, 115
Shelton, Ethel, 53, 100
Simplot, 115
Skyway Luggage, 22
Smith, Ralph, 9, 12, 19
Spokane Spokesman-Review
Spencer, Robert R., 130
Stamets, William K. Jr, 166
Stowell, Ralph, 134
Strain, Douglas C., 168
Street, William S., 56
Stuart, R.W., 57
Sumner Iron Works, 57

Tacoma News Tribune, 21

Taylor, Joseph, 118, 120
Taylor, Moulton, and Aerocar, 32
Tektronix, 96, 115
Texaco refinery,115
Thurman, Stan, 154
Tide, 18
Timber Structures, 47
Tips on Trips, 22
Tongue, Gordon, 168
Tradepapers, 12, 27
Tri-City Herald, 31
Truex, G. Robert Jr, 134-136

Ulrich, W.J., 165
Union Pacific, 116
United Control, 96, 115
U.S. National Bank, 88, 90, 96
U.S. Oil & Refining, 115
U.S. Plywood, Texas mill, 124
U.S. Steel Supply, 46
Uranium ore, 115

Vancouver Columbian, 21
Vander Ende, Gerrit, 151

Wakefield, A.A, 46
Waldorf Paper, 115
Walker's Weekly Newsletter, 118
Wall Street Journal, 85
Walters, D.W., 46
Walthers, Ralph V., 166
Washington Mutual, 64, 93, 153
Welch, William E., 47

West Coast Fast Freight, 55
West Coast Lumbermen's Assn, 72
Western Kraft, 76, 115
Western Union, 25-26
Westvaco, 115.
Weyerhaeuser, 21, 46, 74, 115, 116, 150
Whitman estate, 114
Willamette Industries, 64, 150
Winlock, WA, 59
Wilson, C.A., 78
Wollenberg, R.P., 169
Woodbury, Sid, 166

Young, Charles, 74